Coloring Garbage Trucks

Garbage Truck Coloring Book

Jupiter Kids

JUPITER KIDS
CHILDREN'S & KIDS FICTION

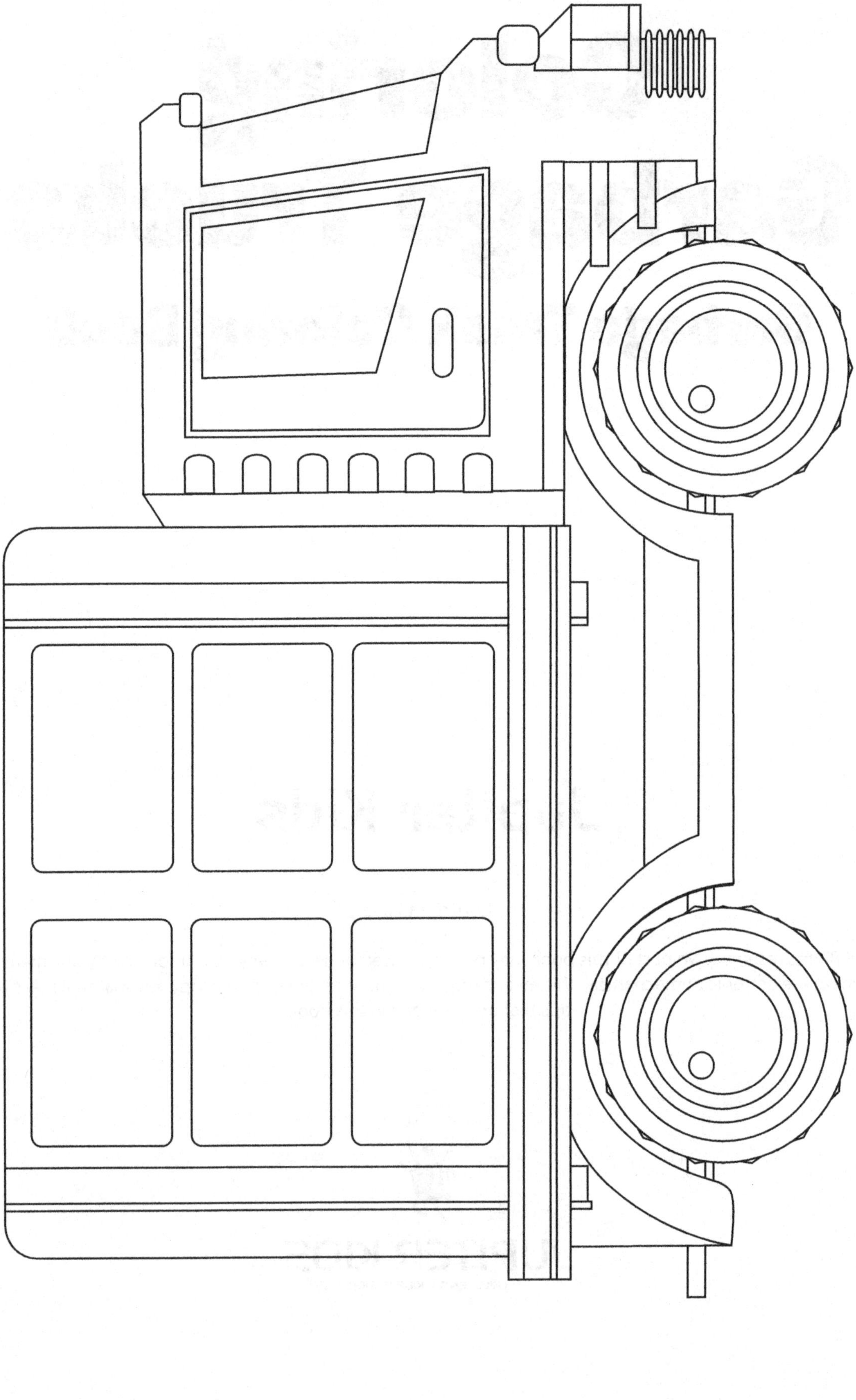

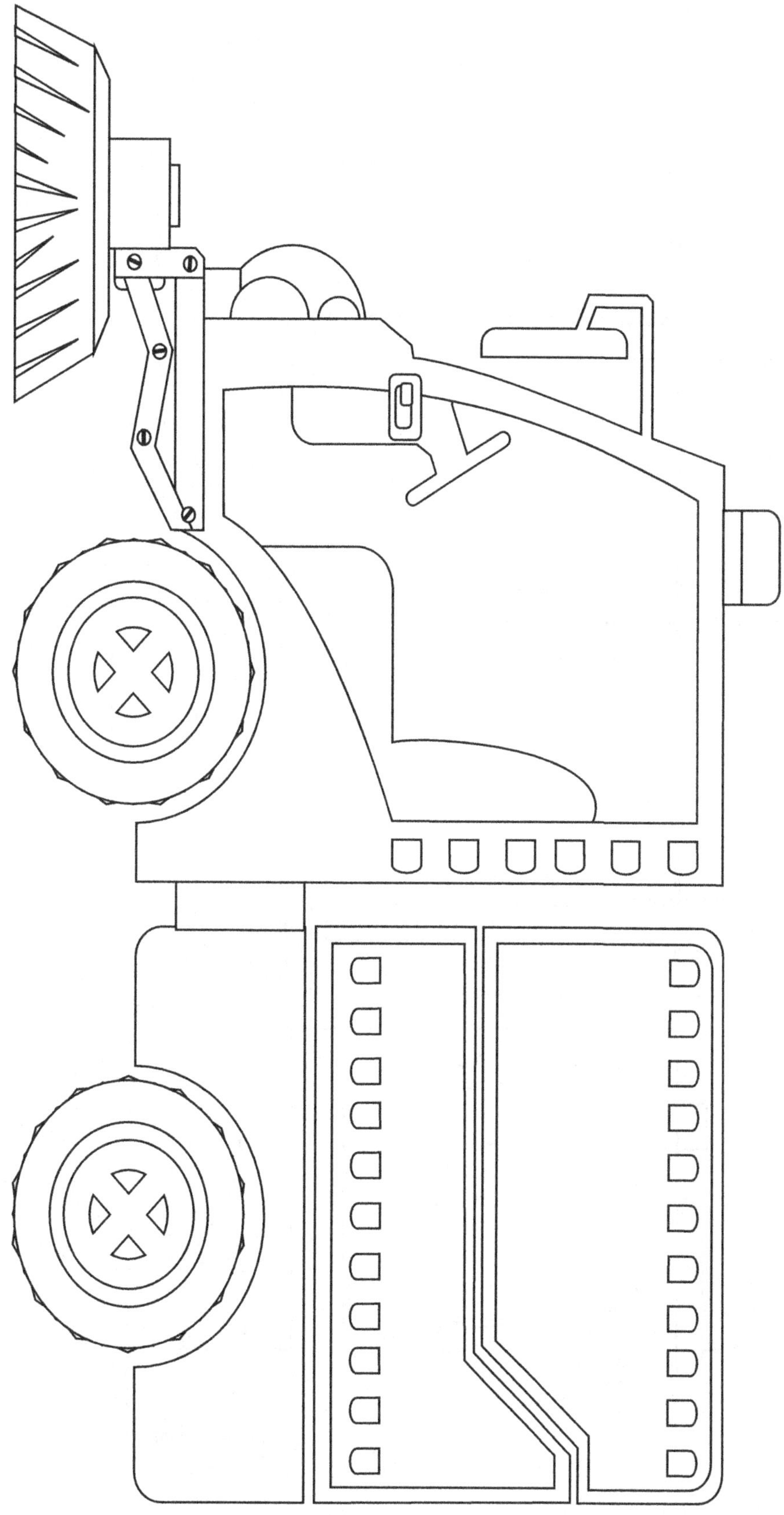

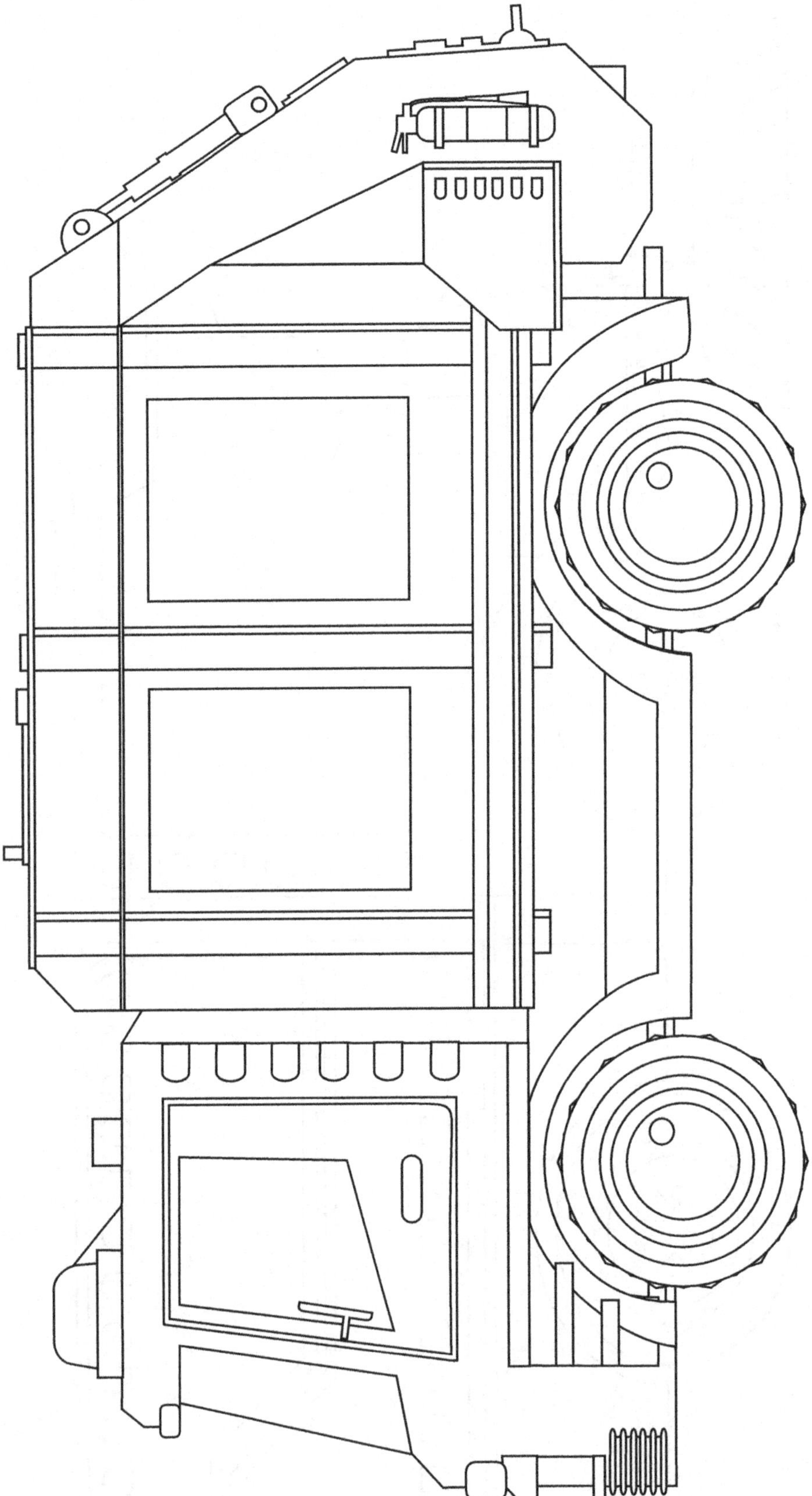

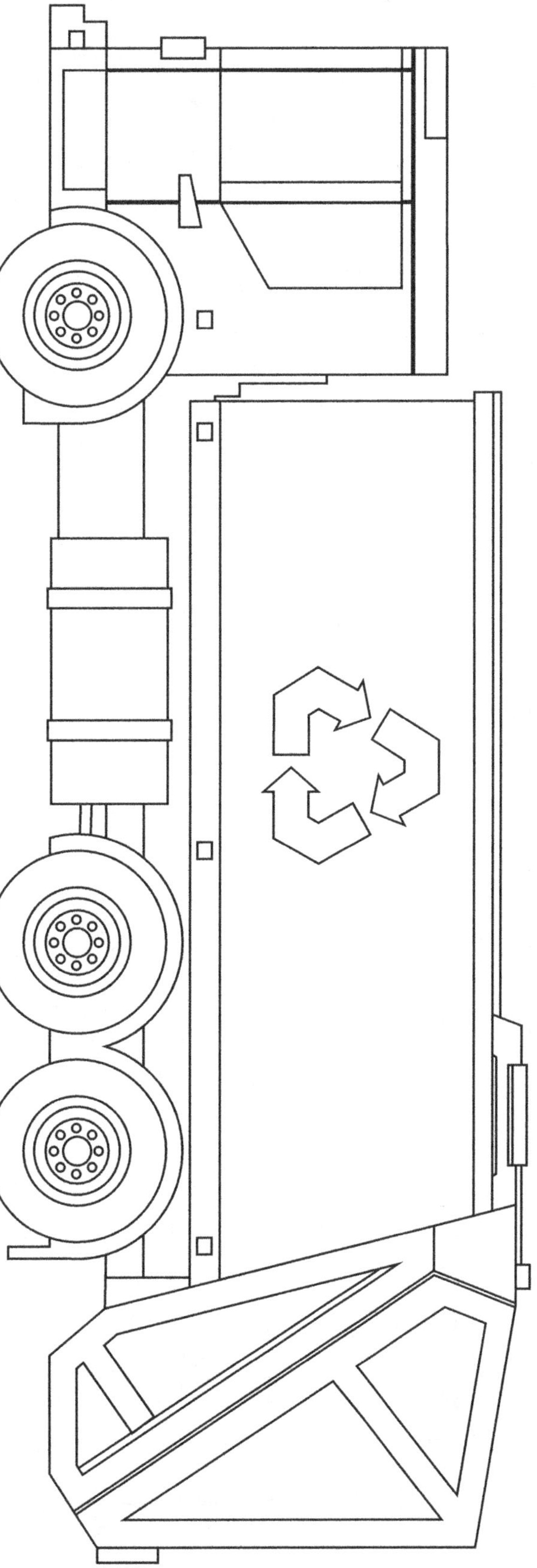

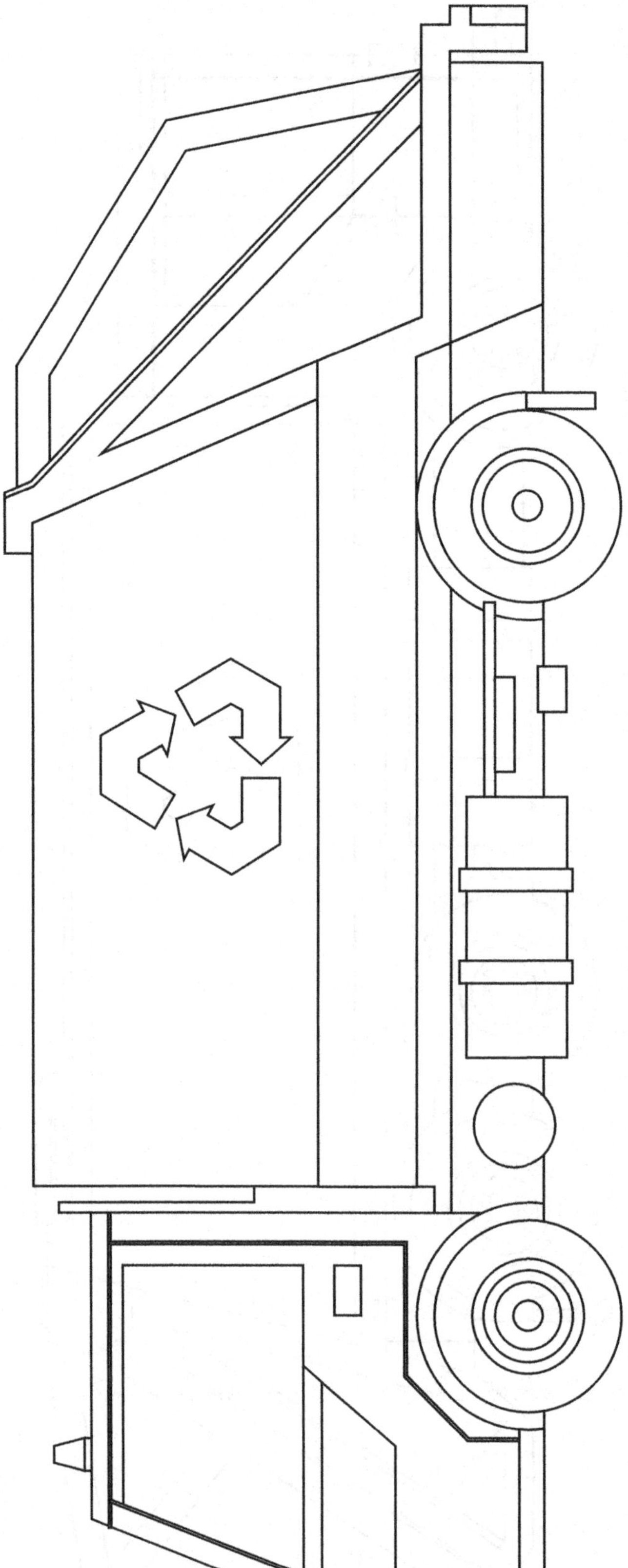

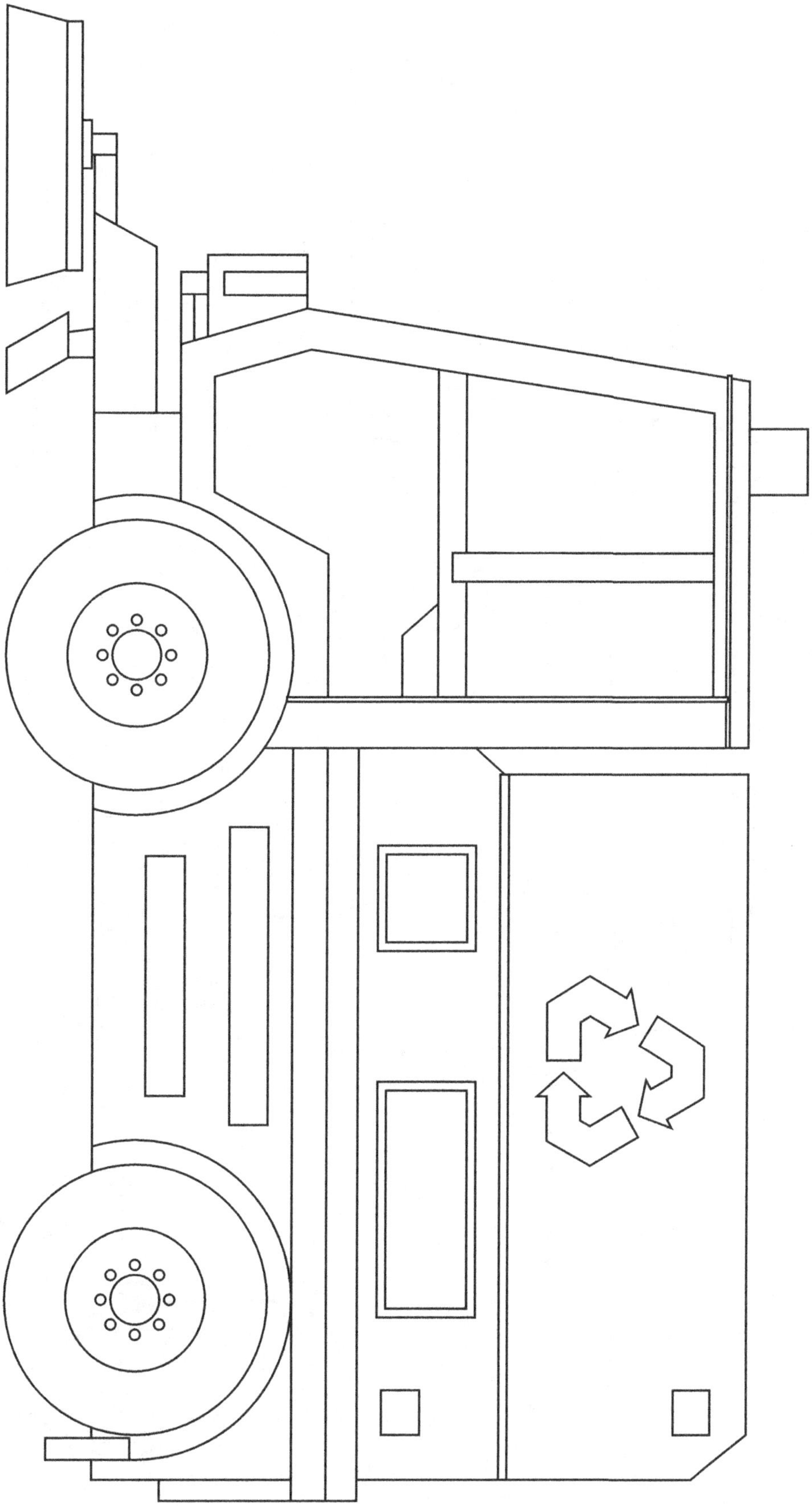

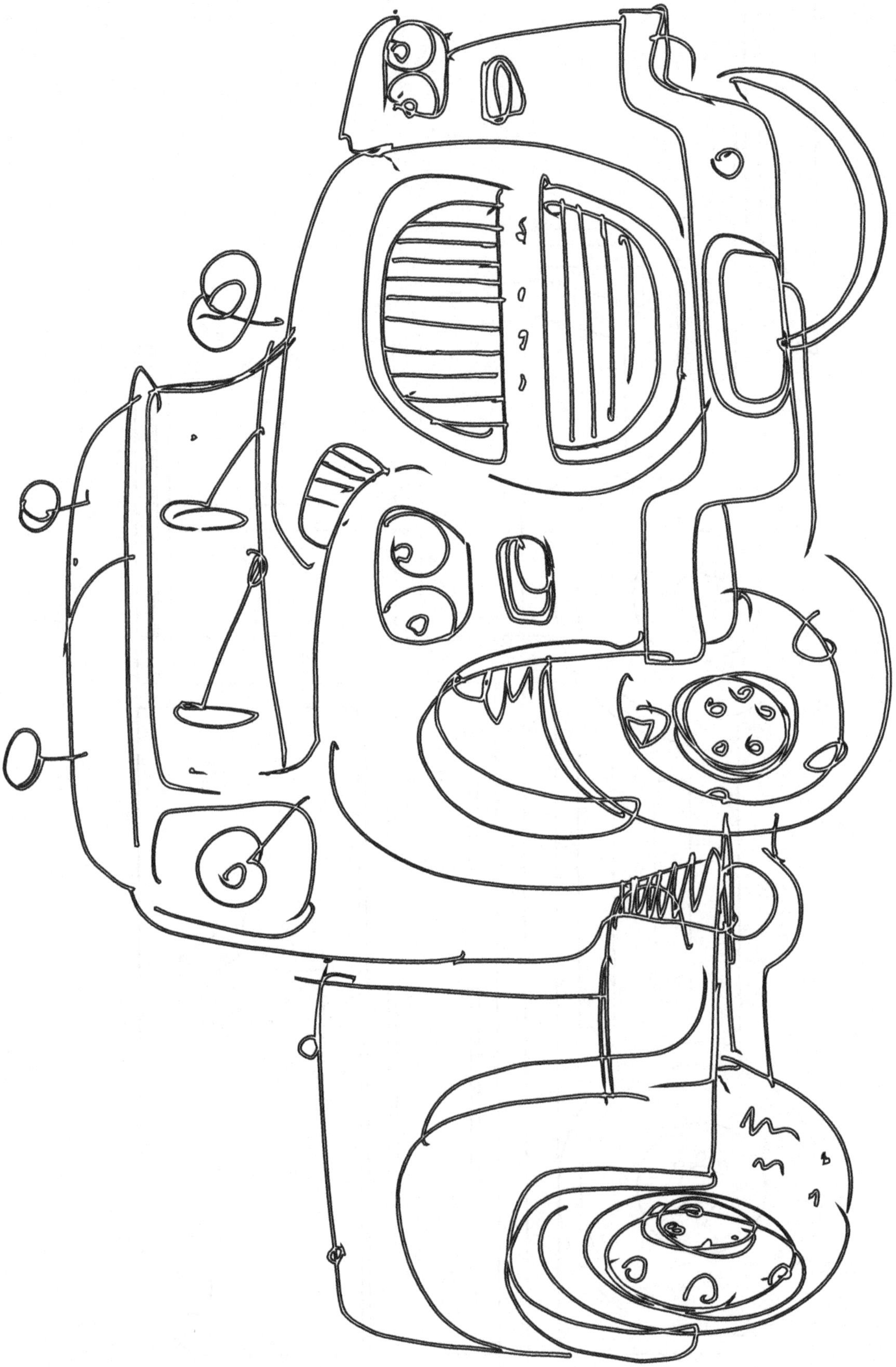

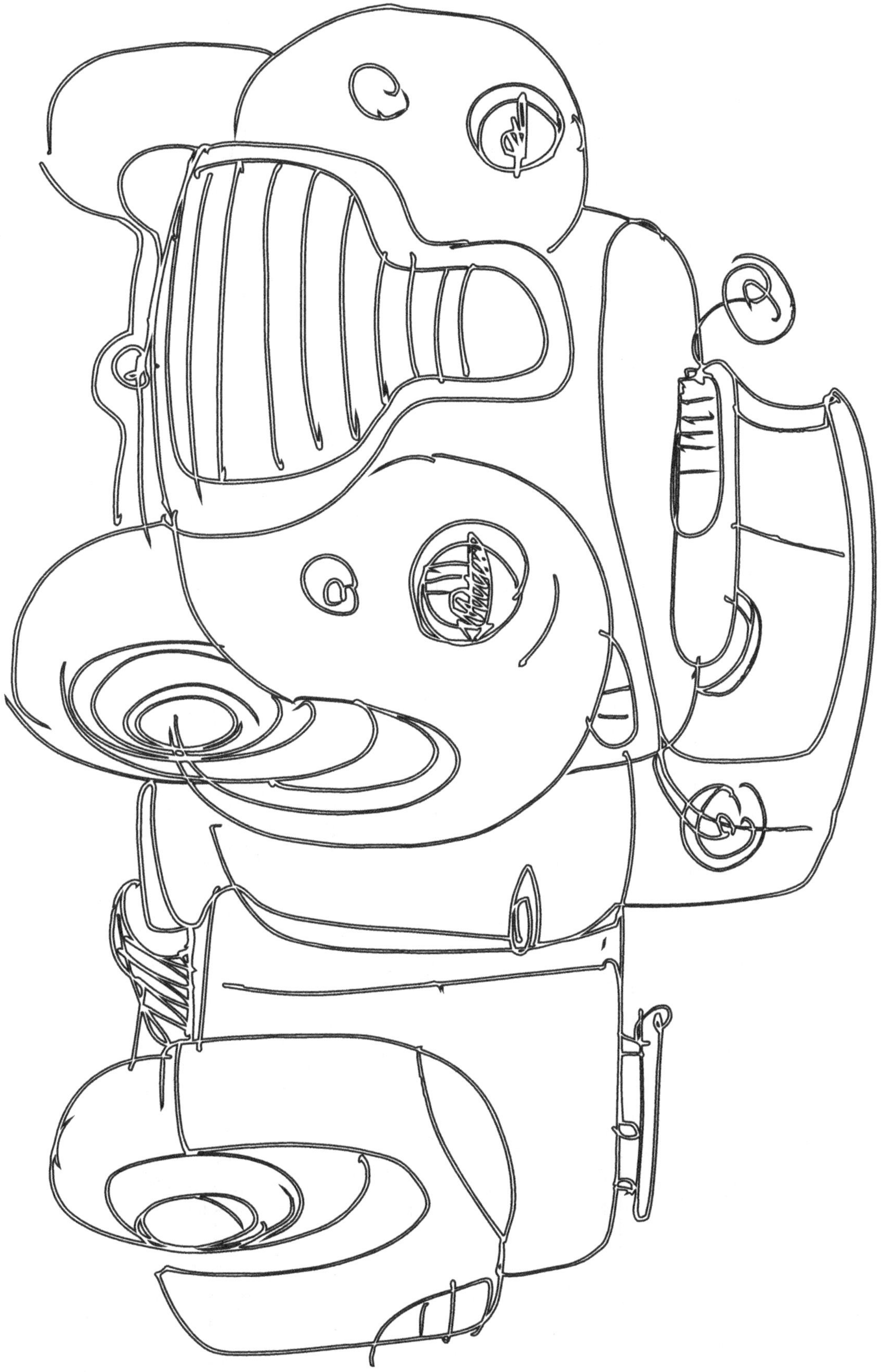

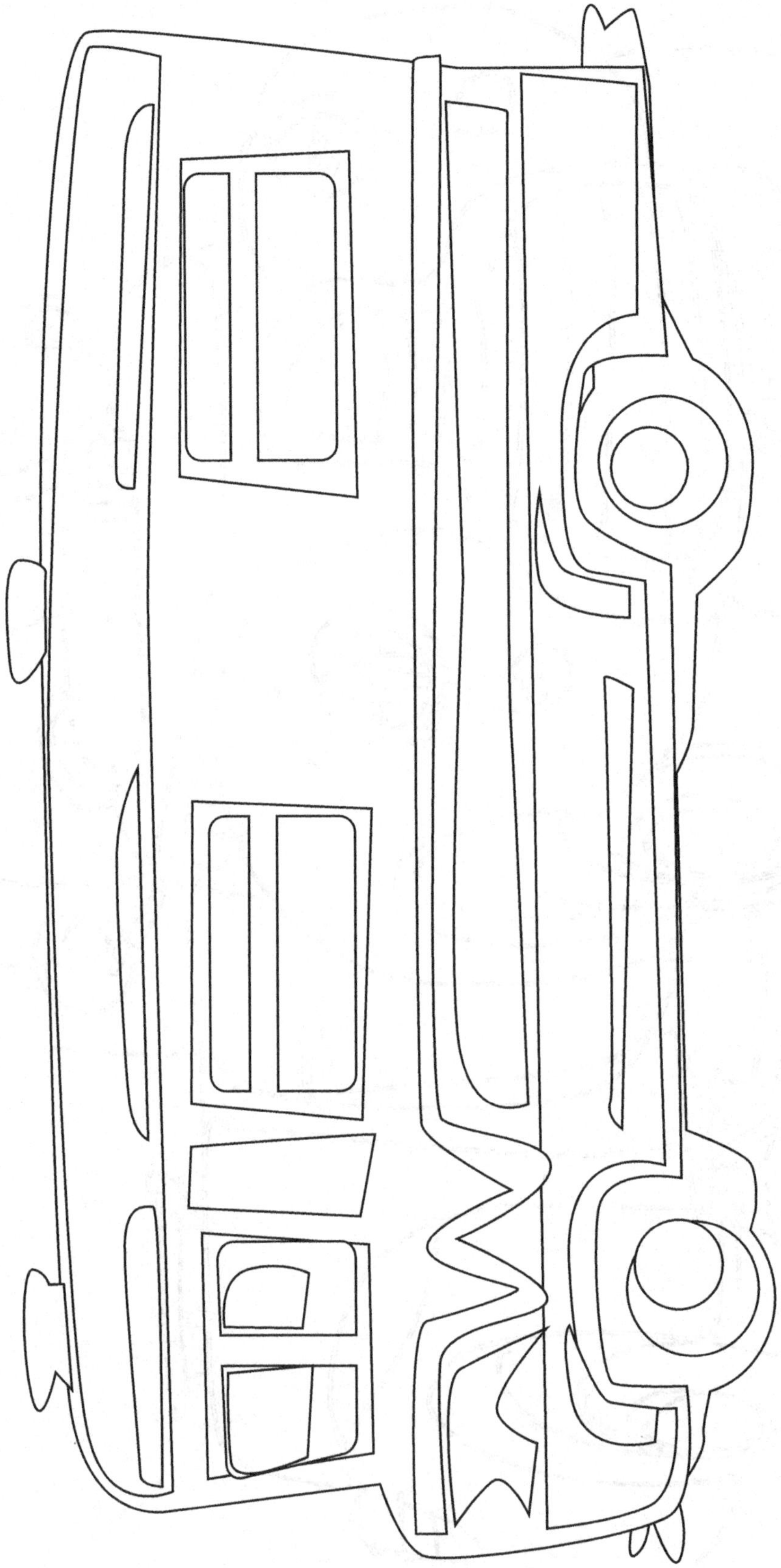

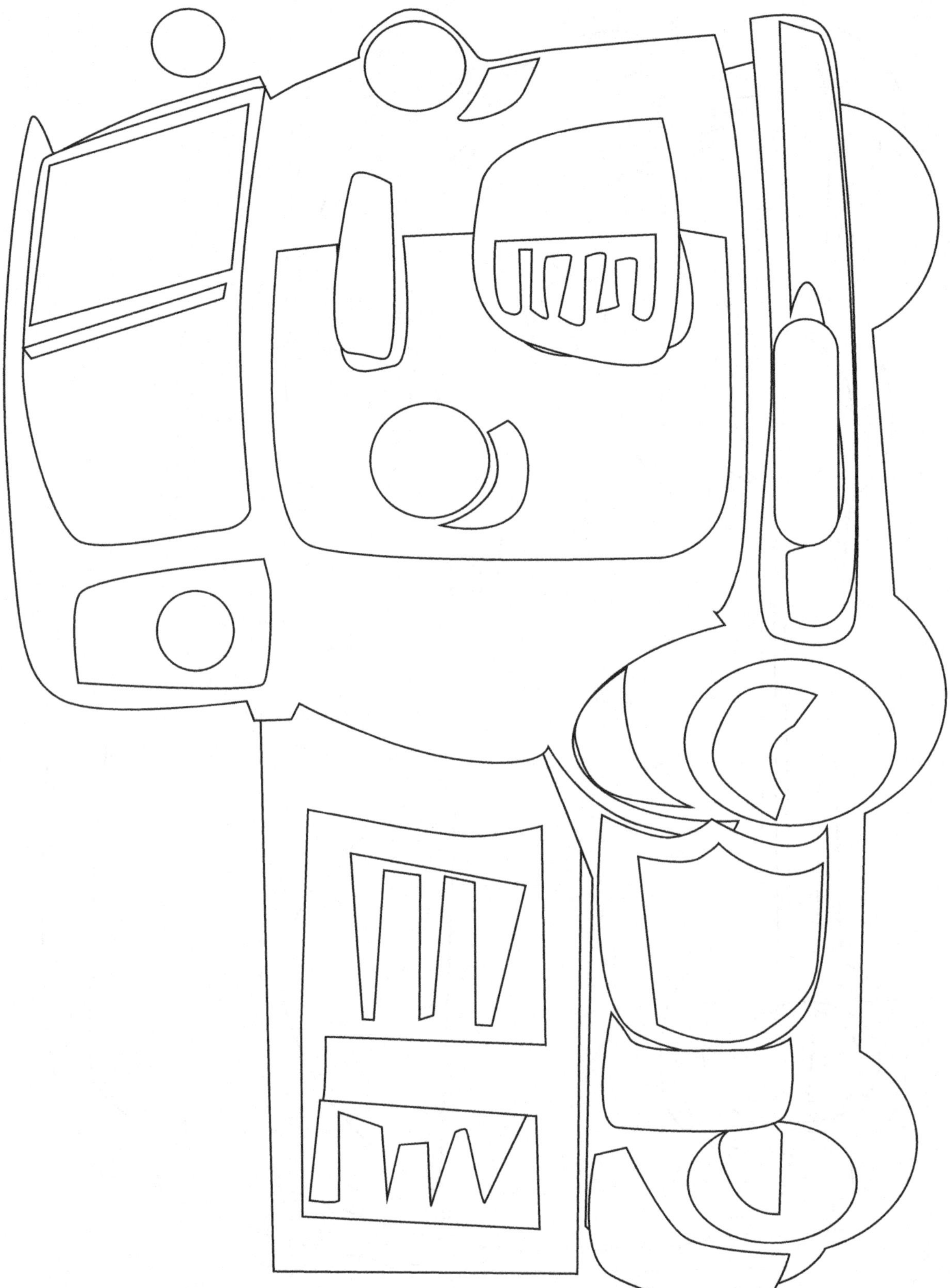

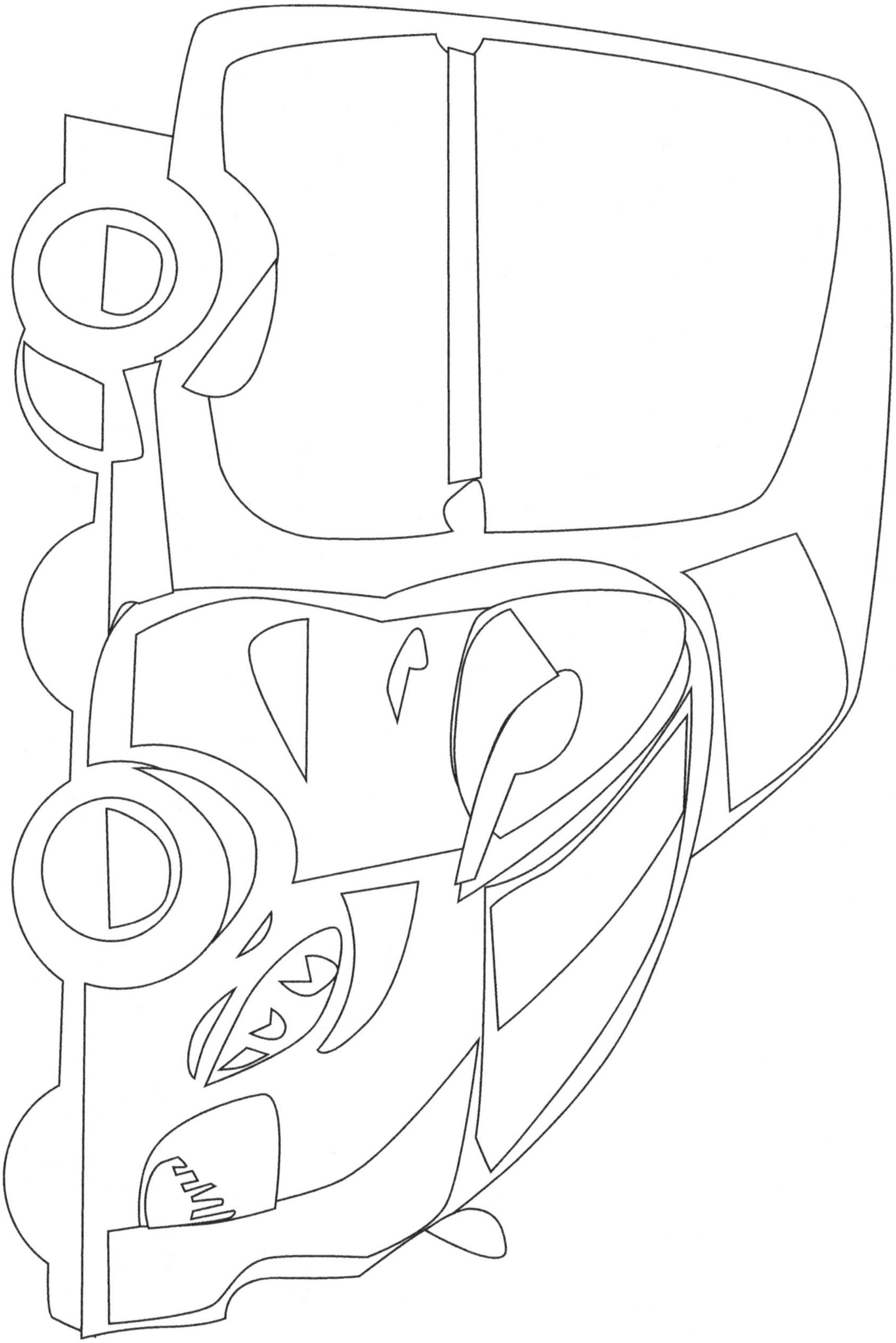

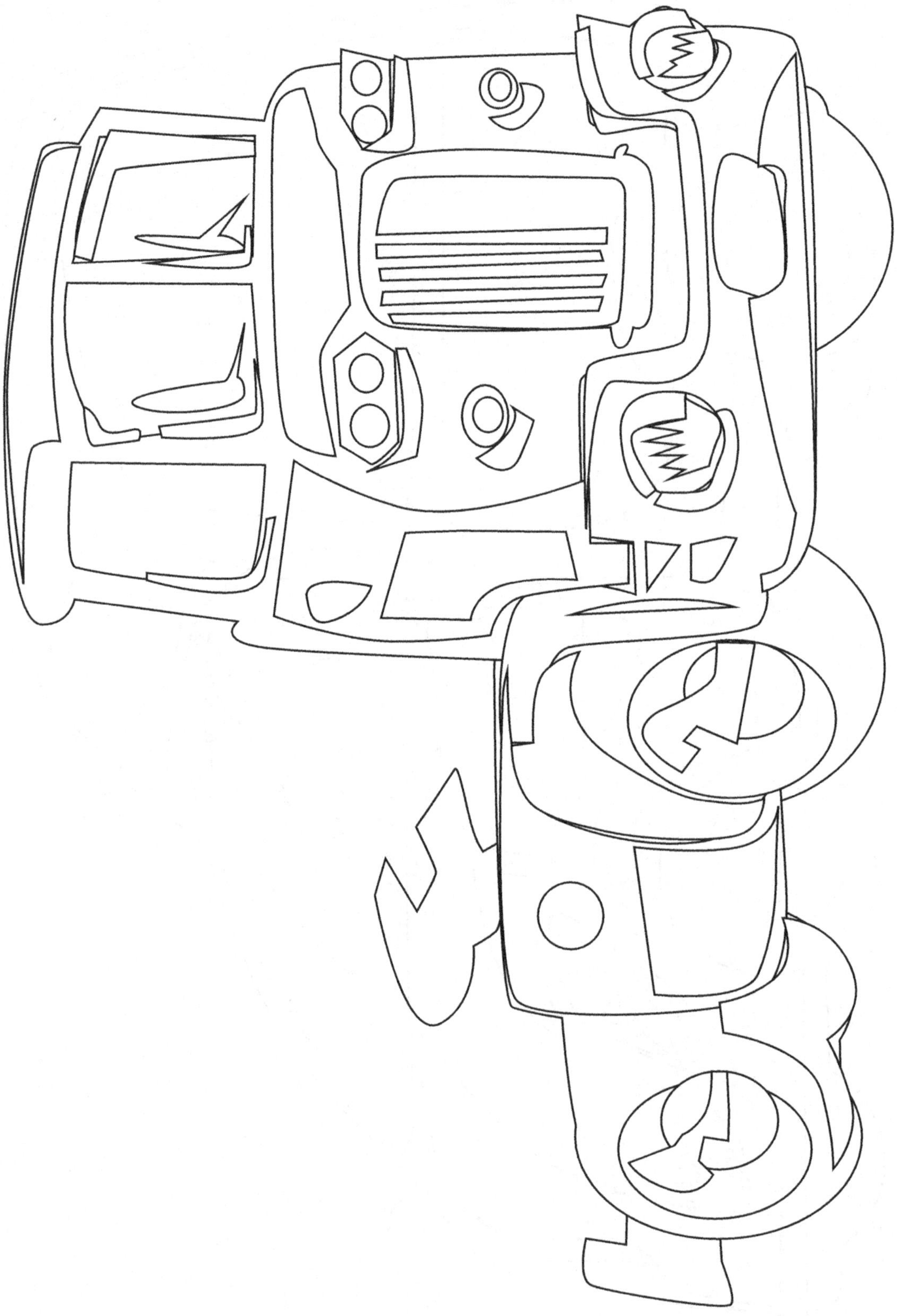

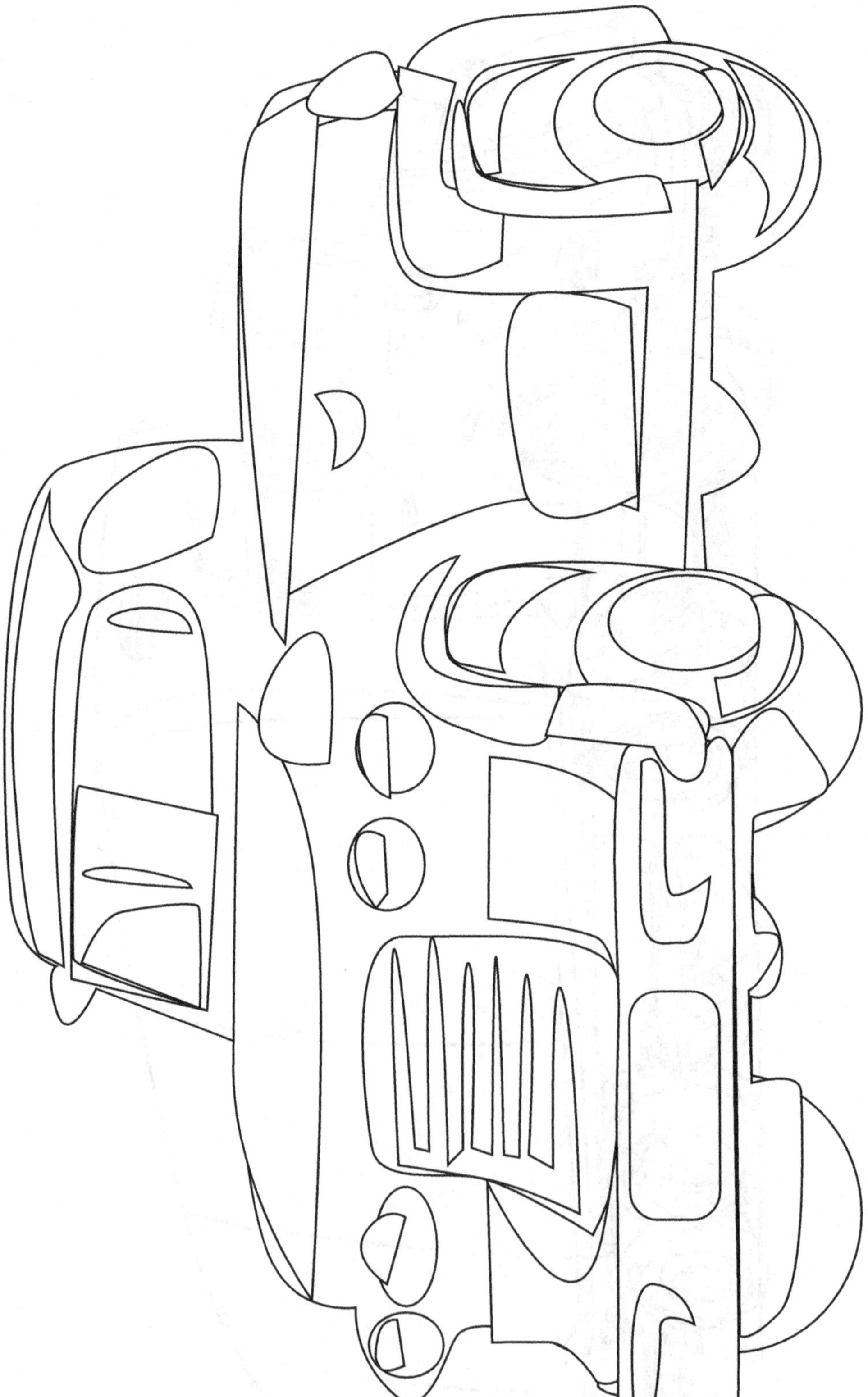

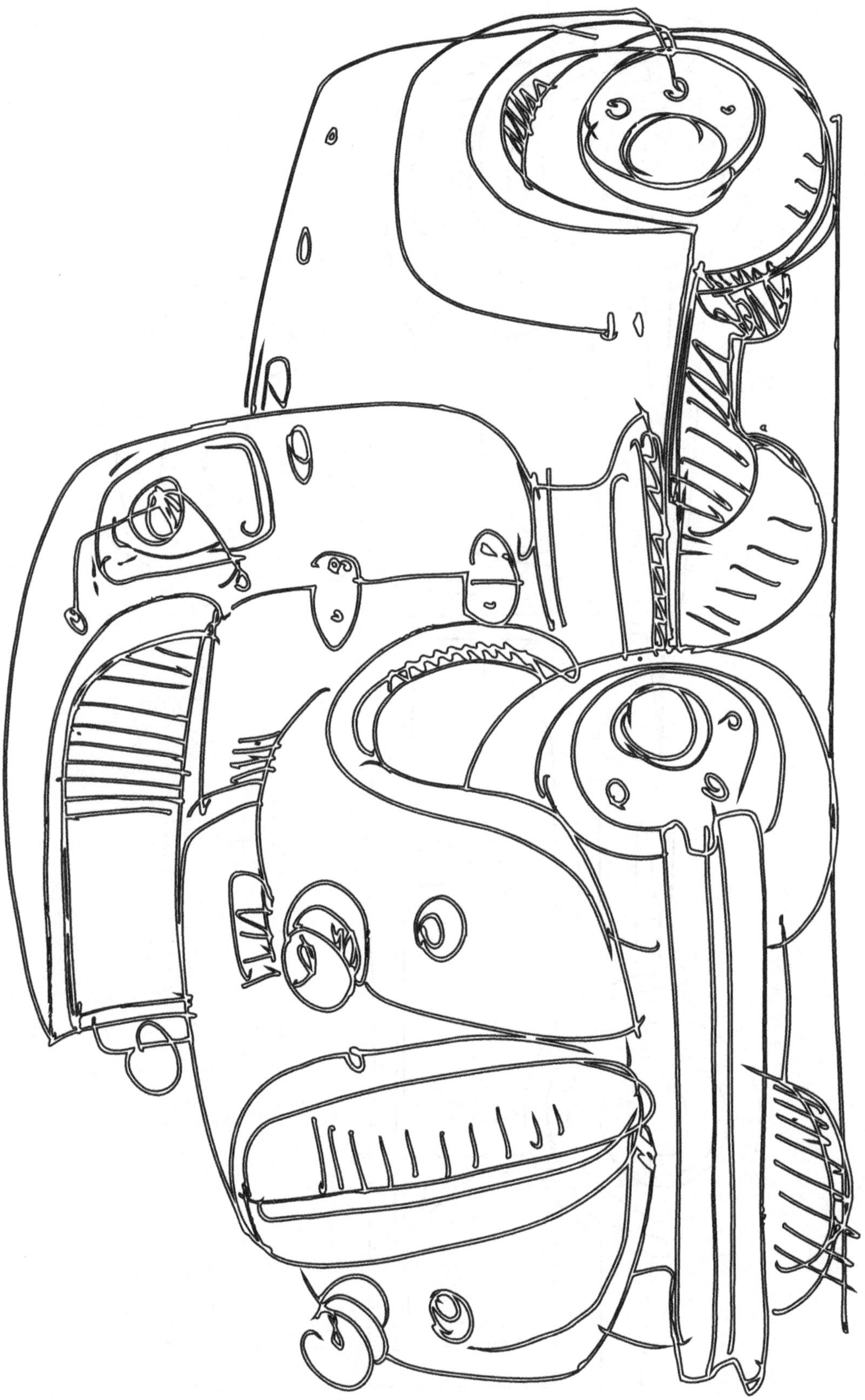

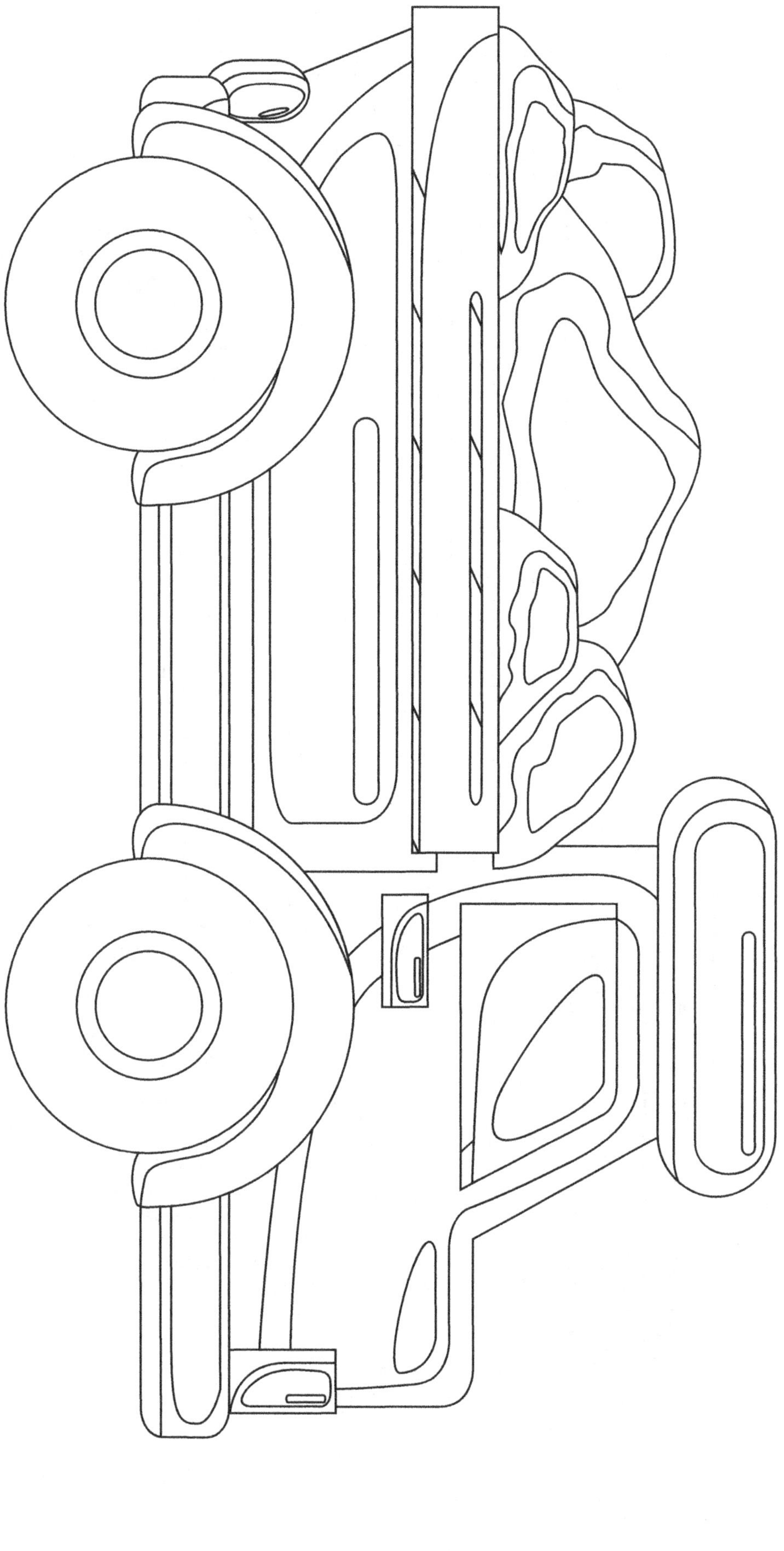

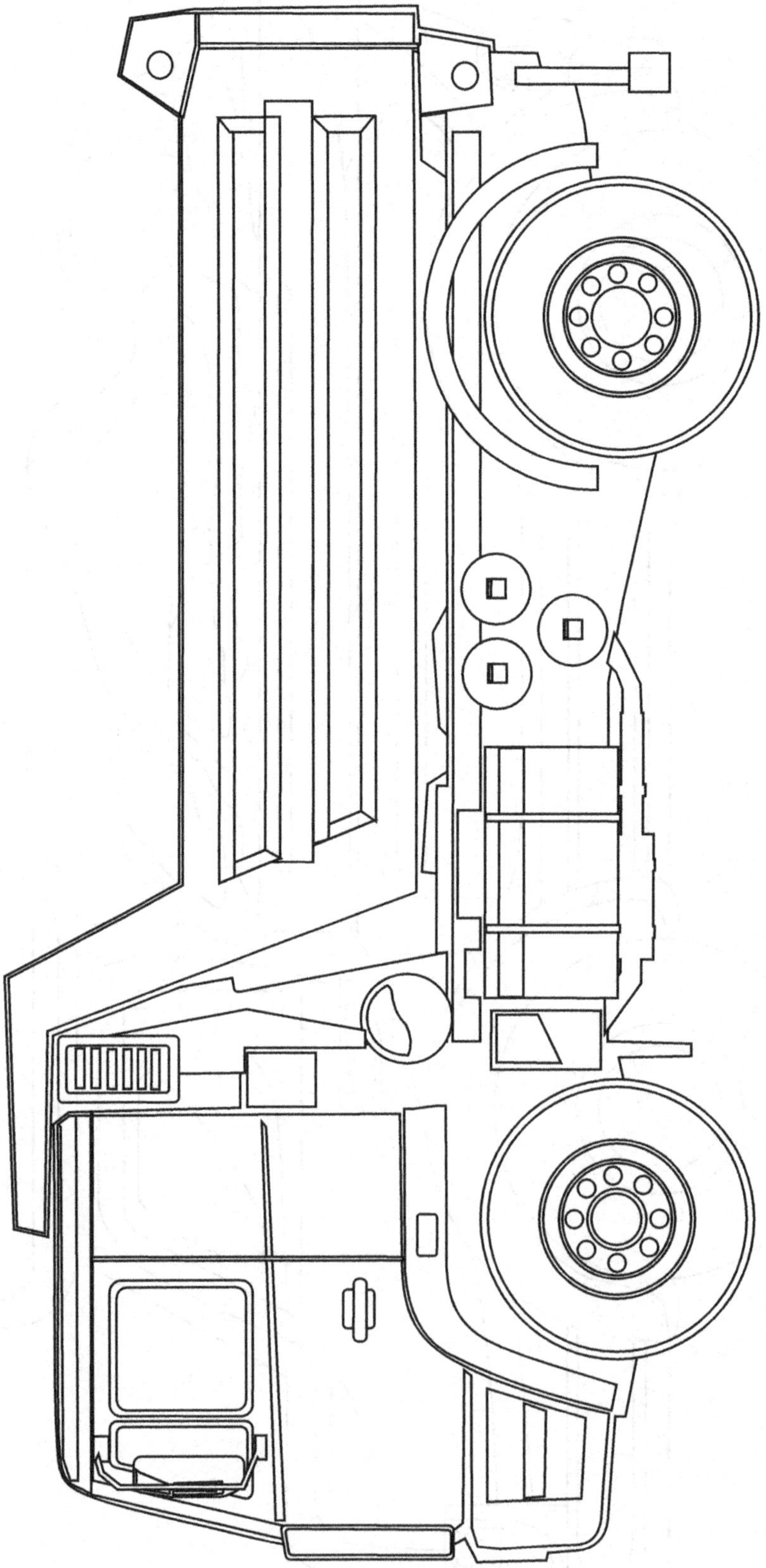

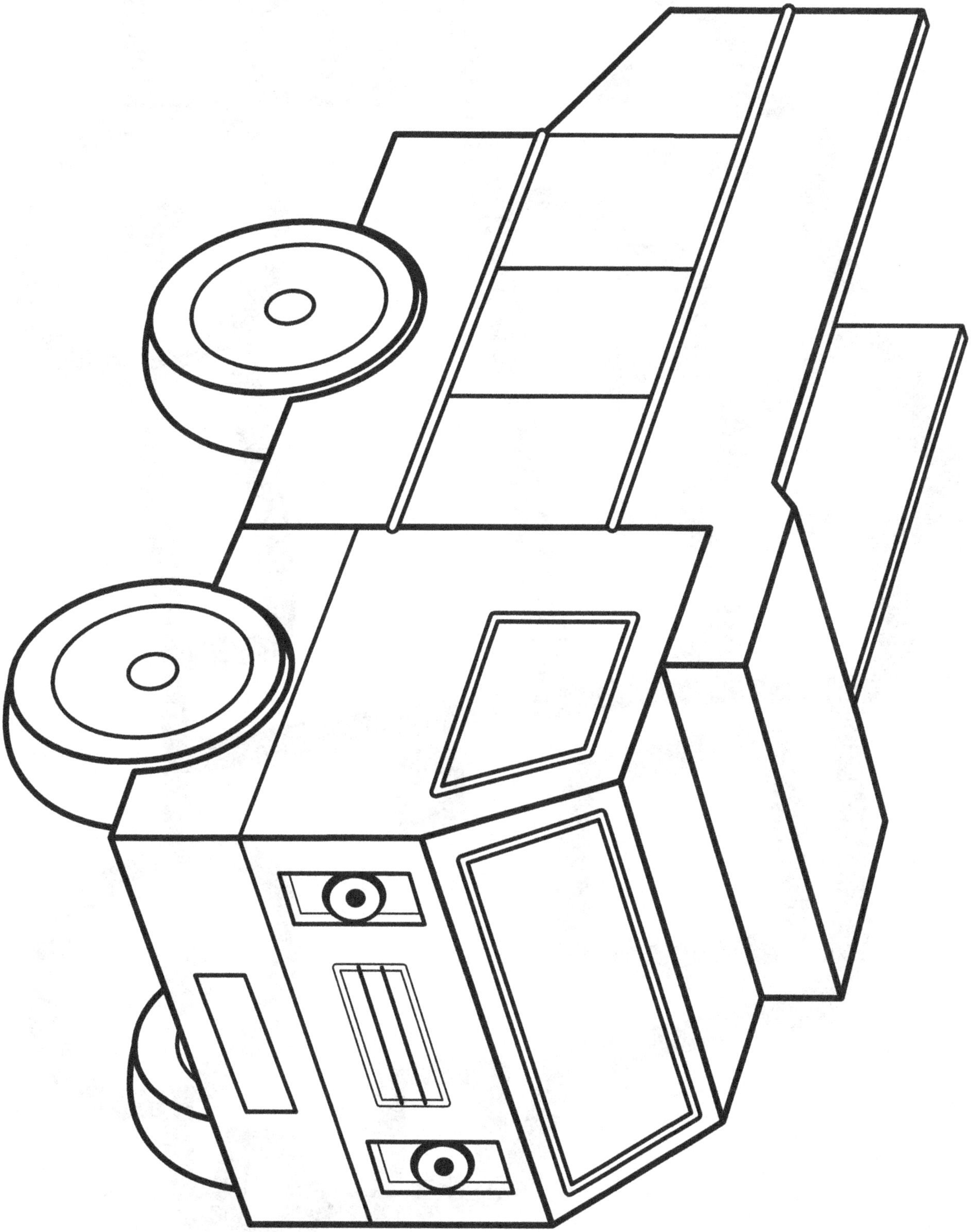

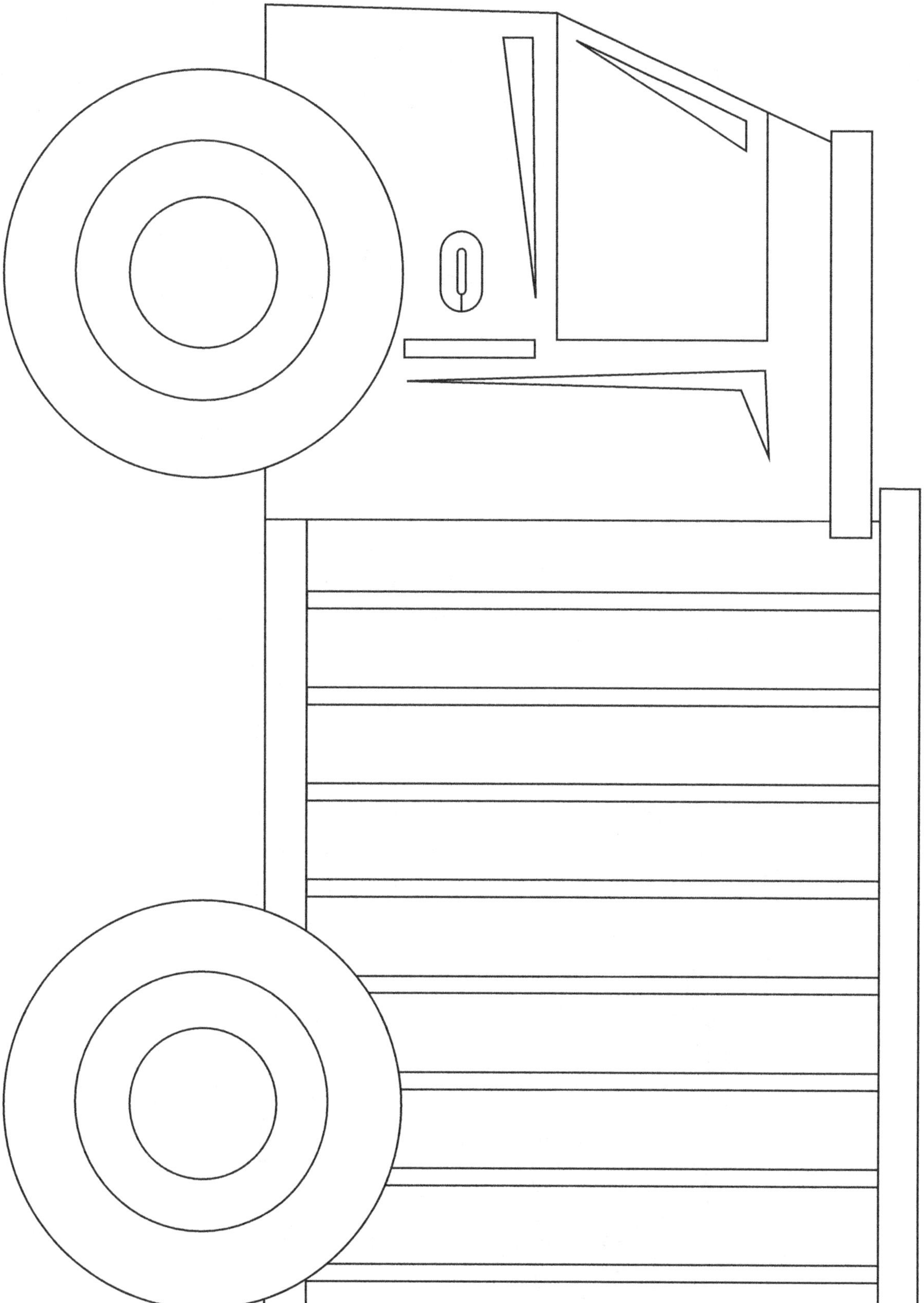

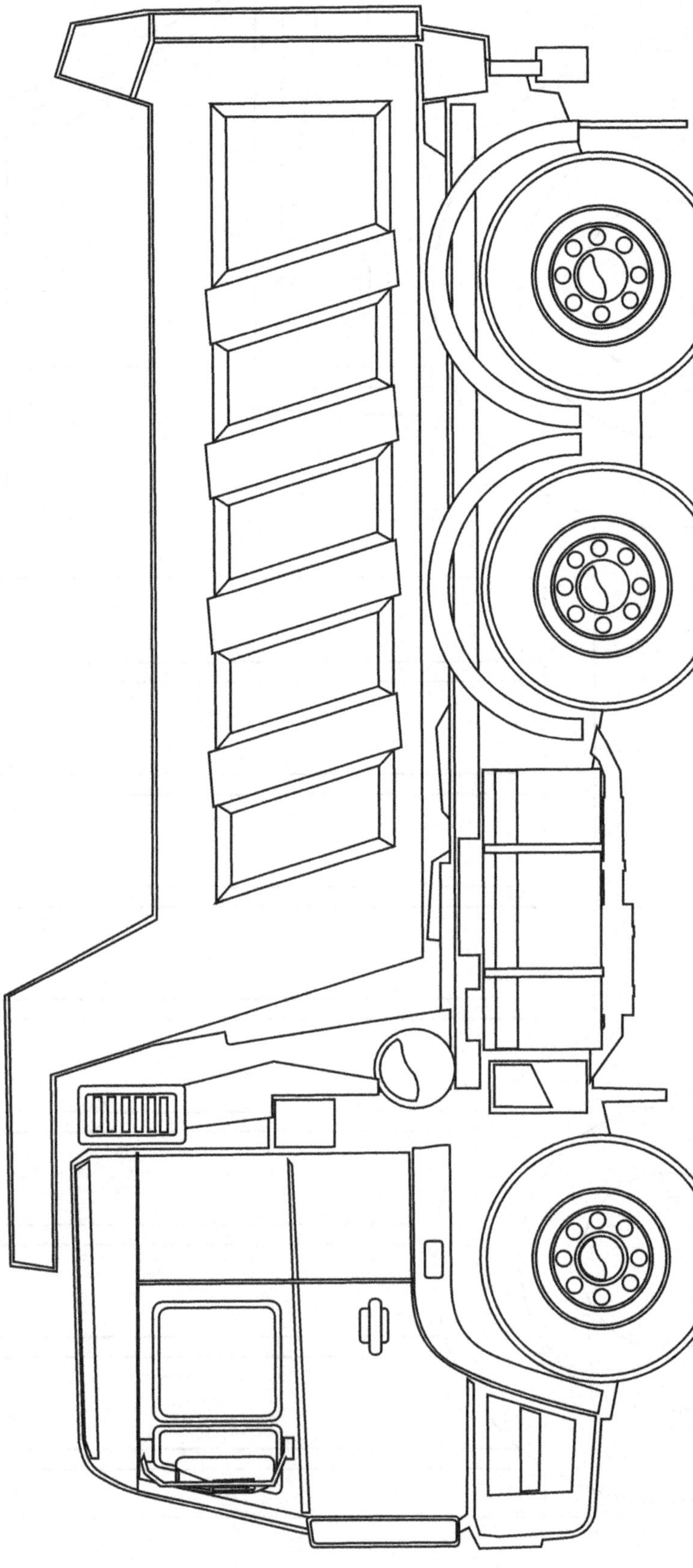

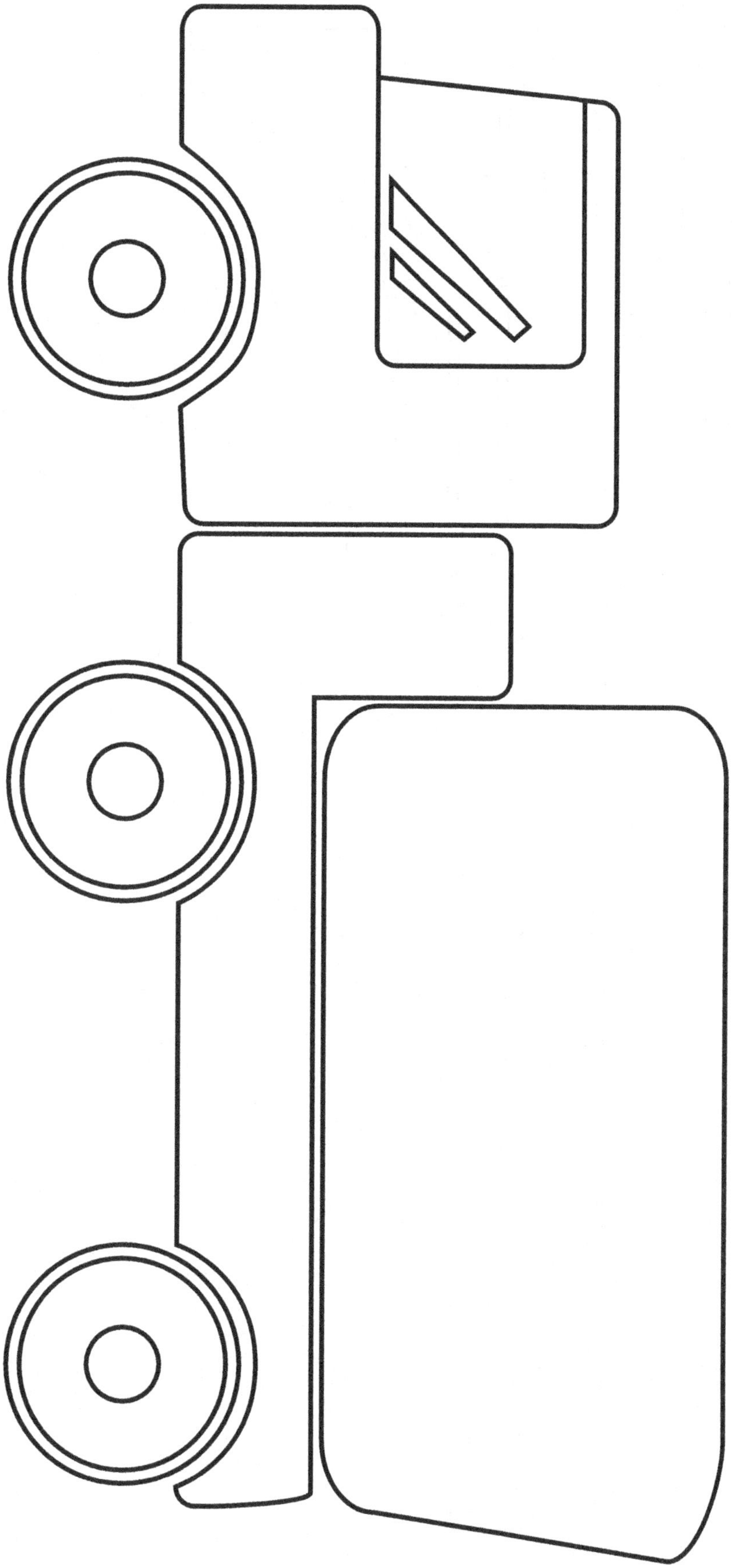

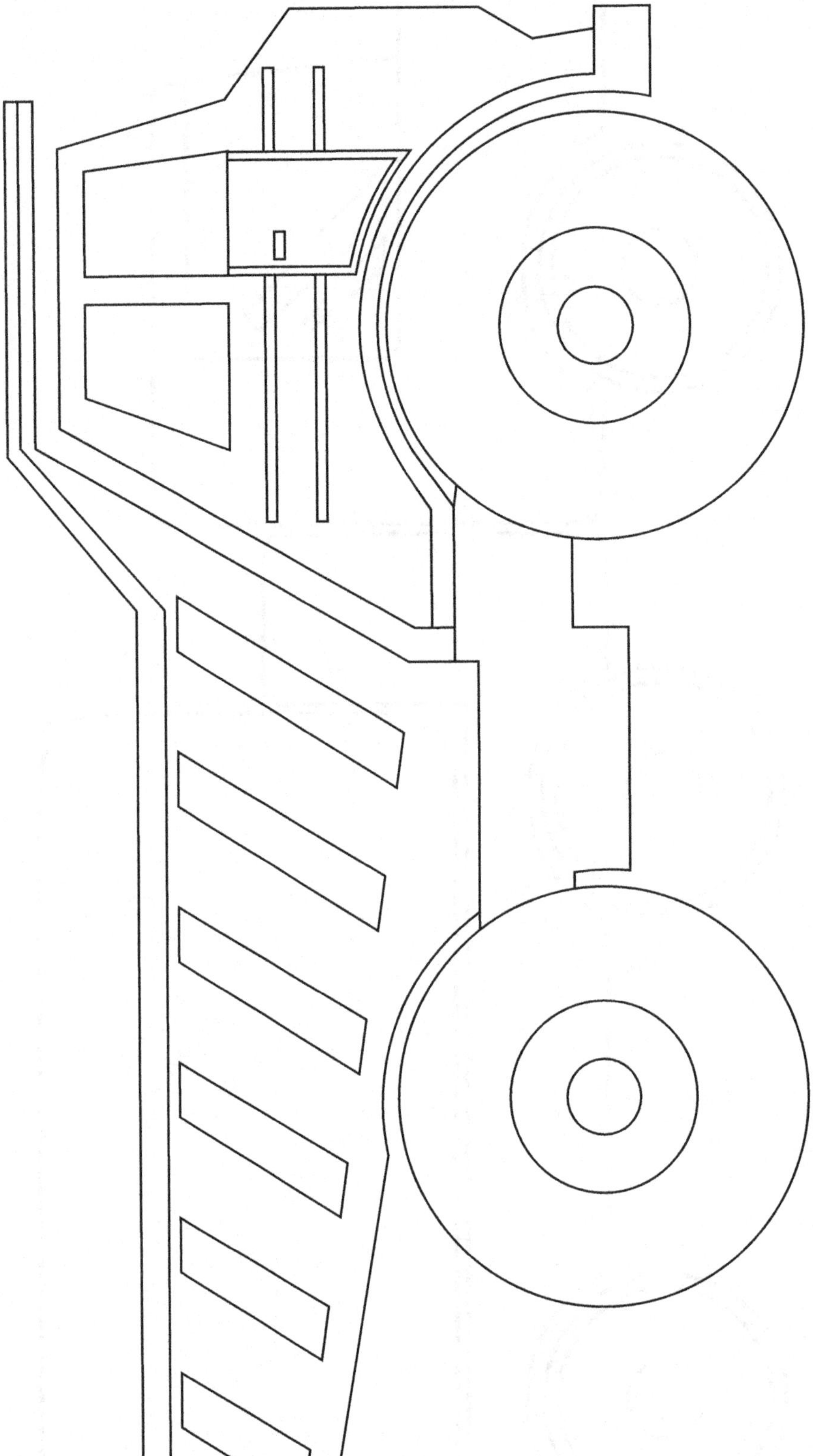

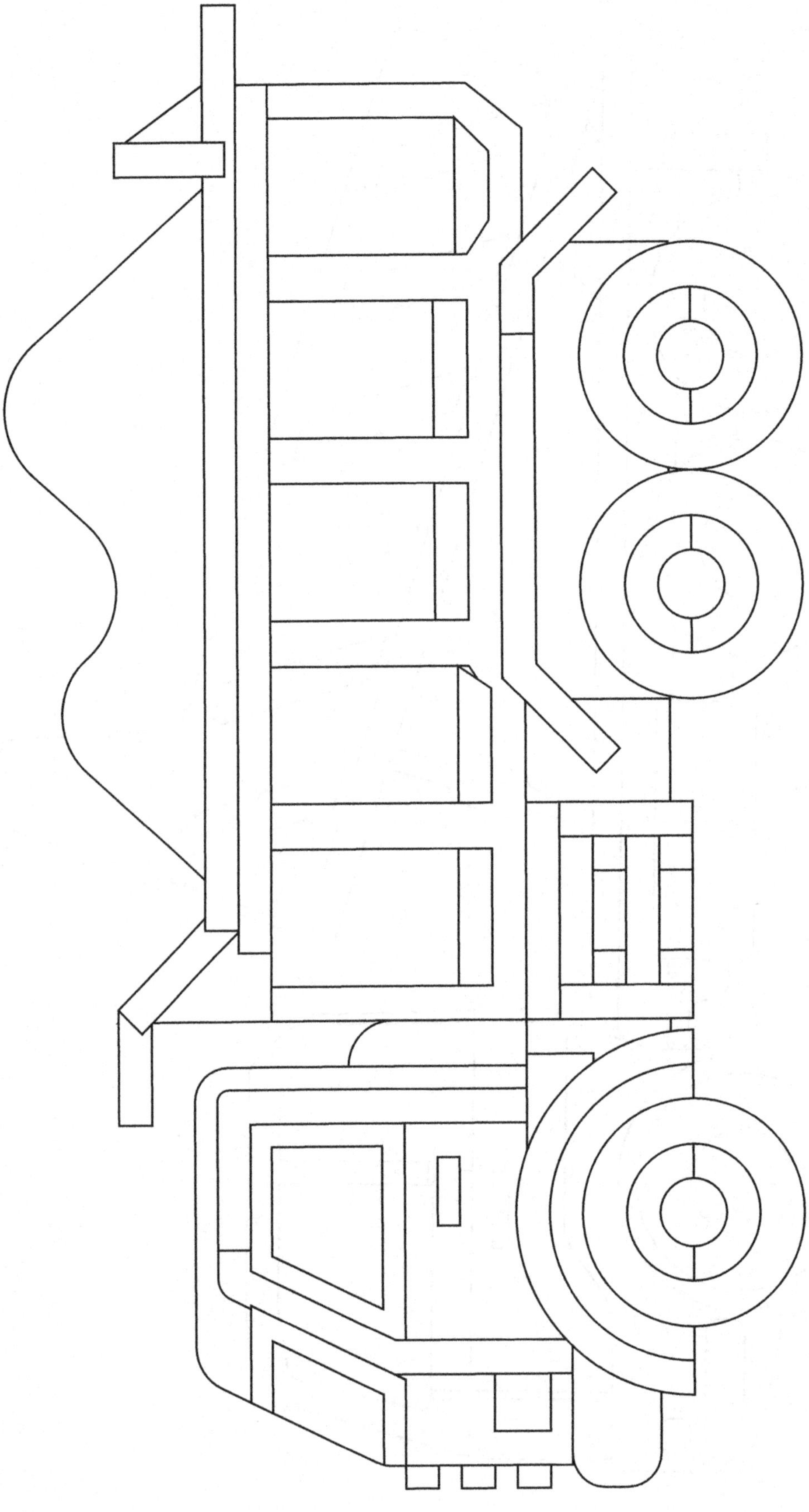

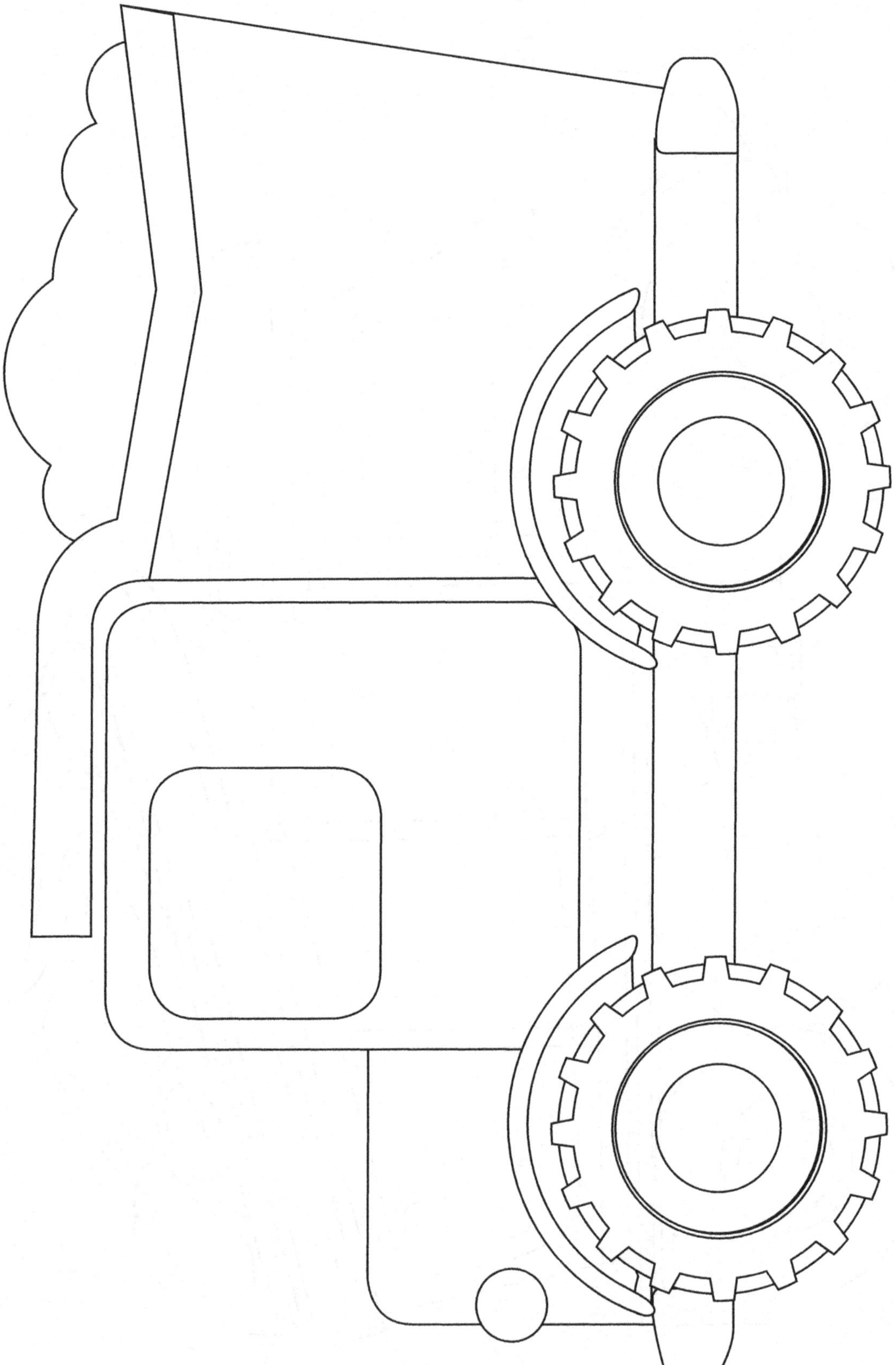

Continue the coloring fun! Here are some more heavy-duty vehicles to color!

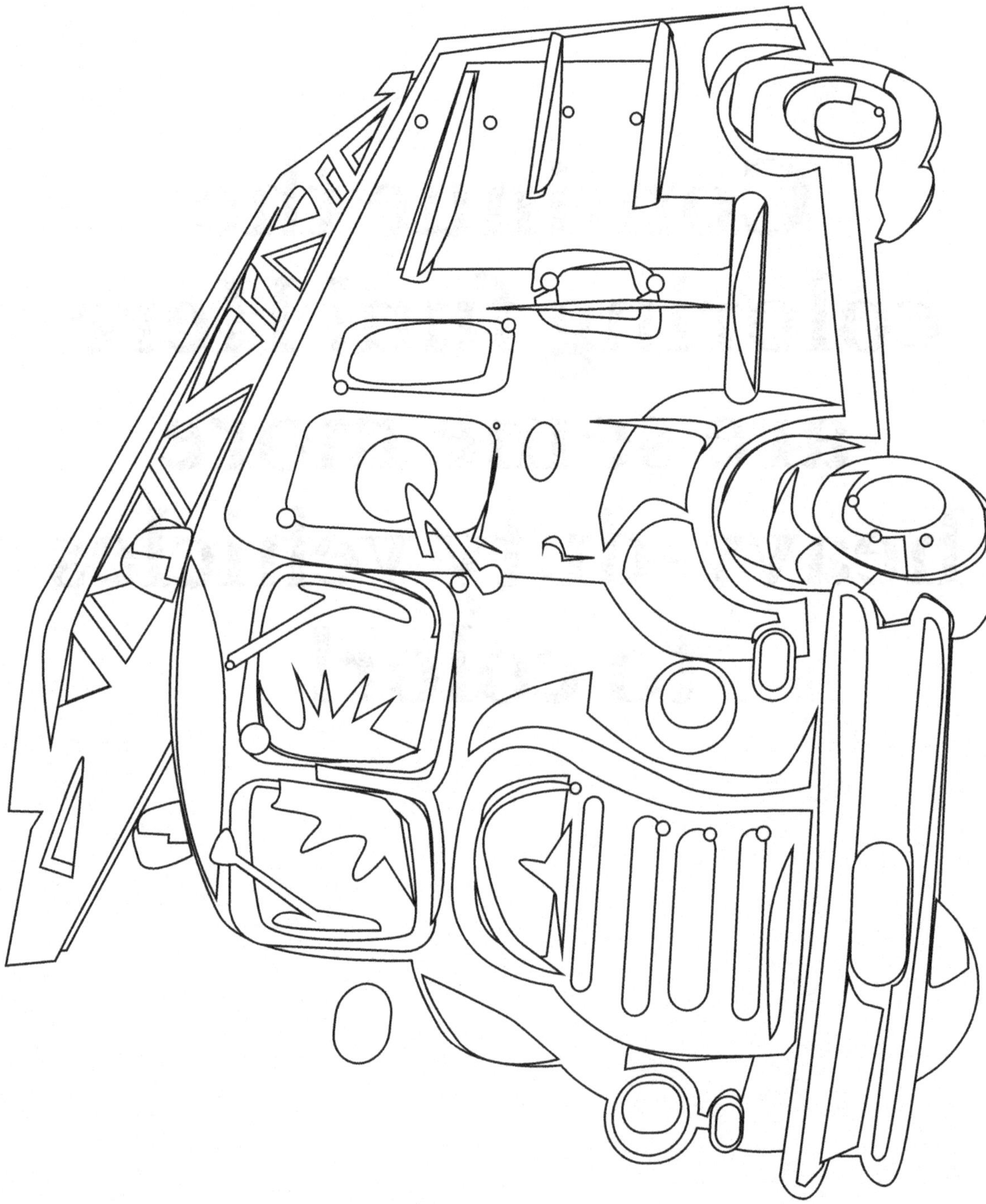

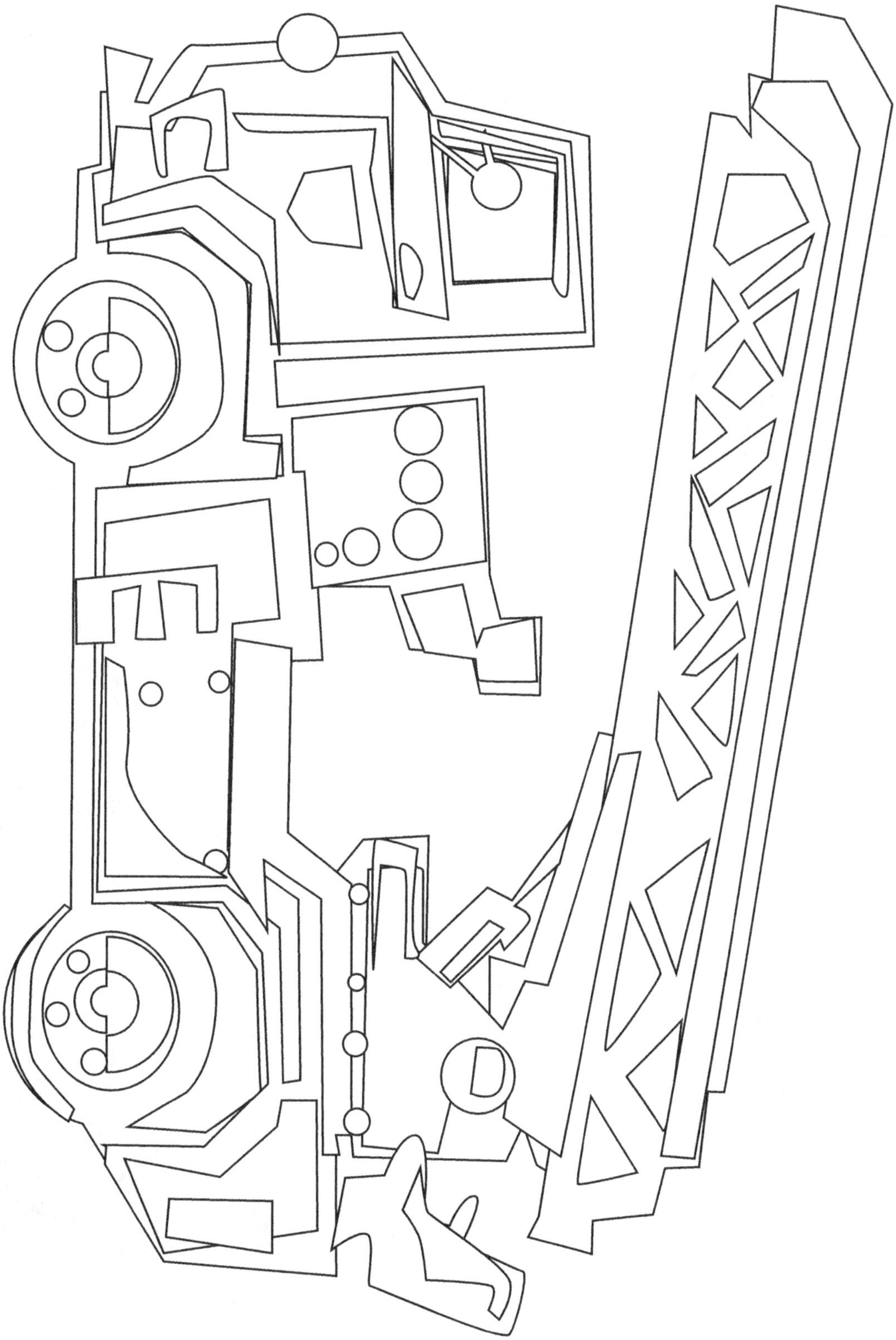

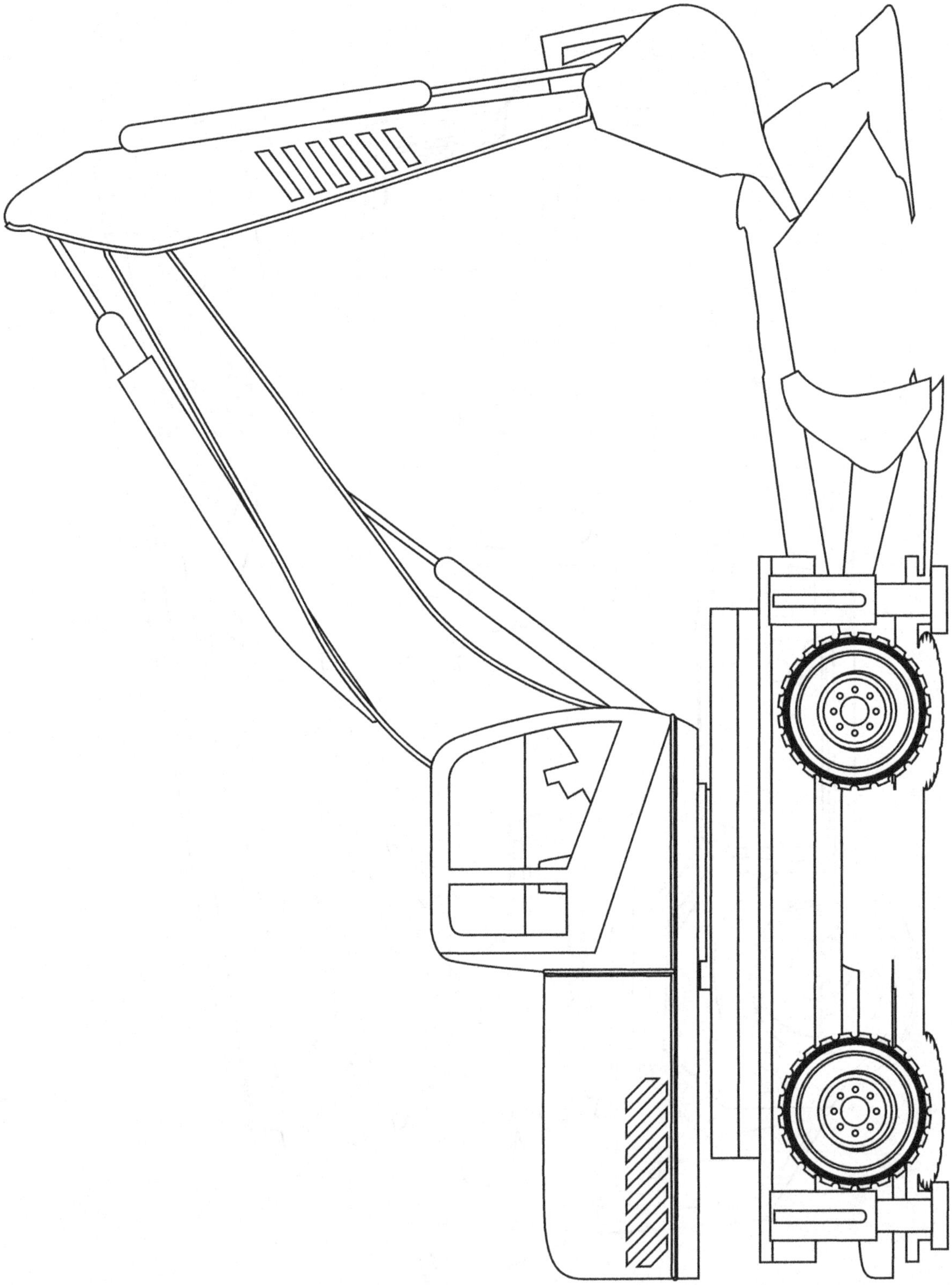

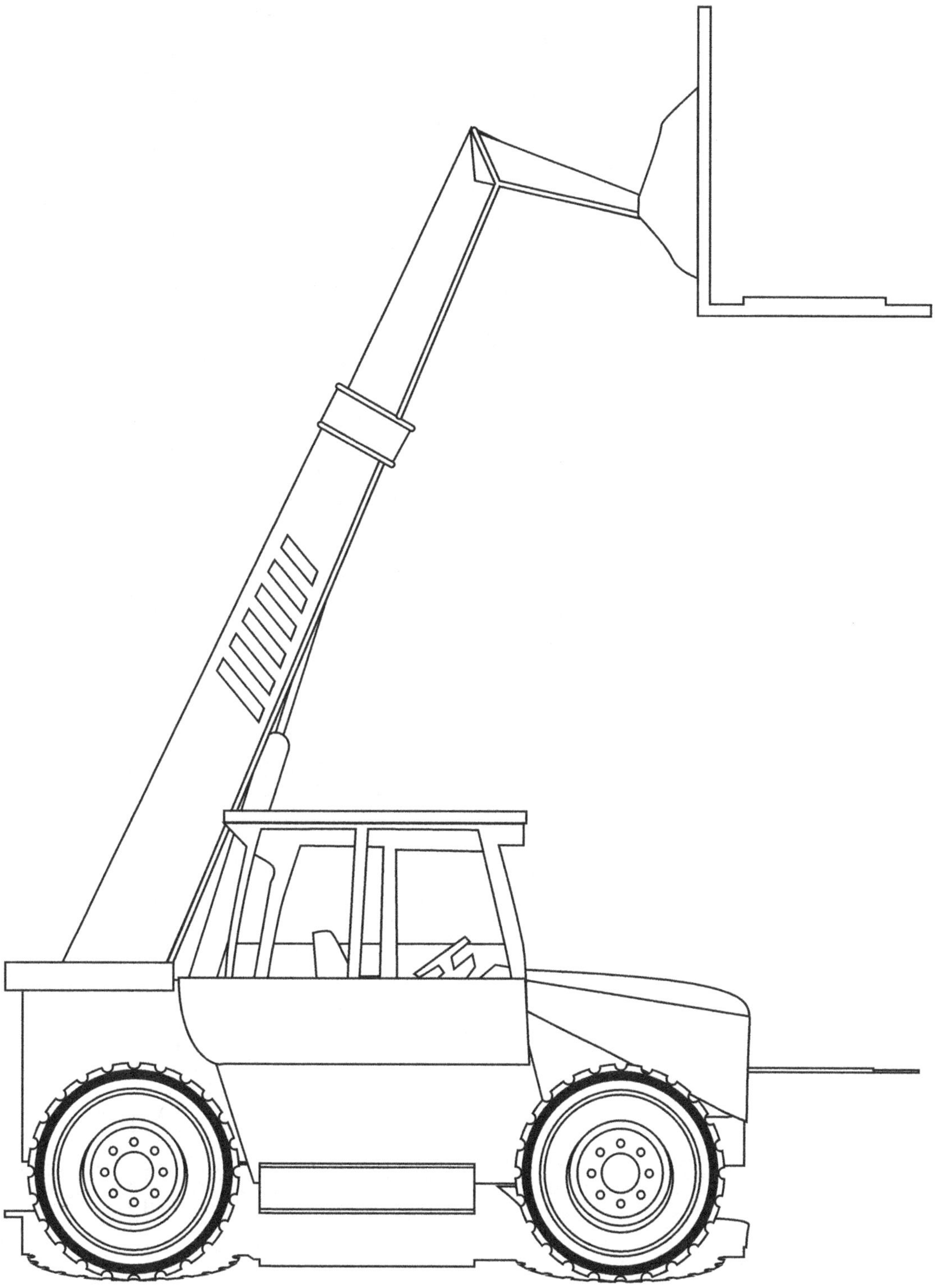

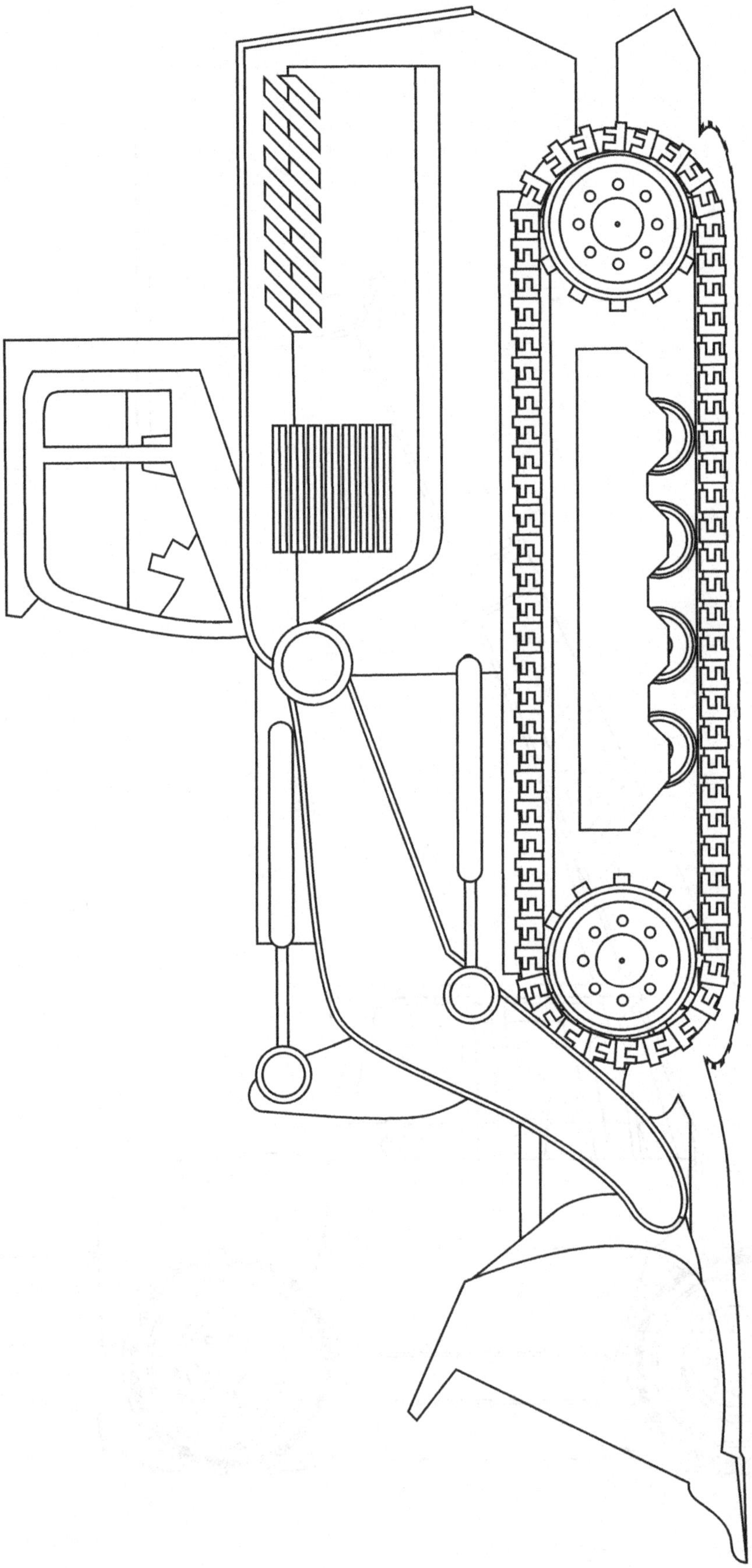

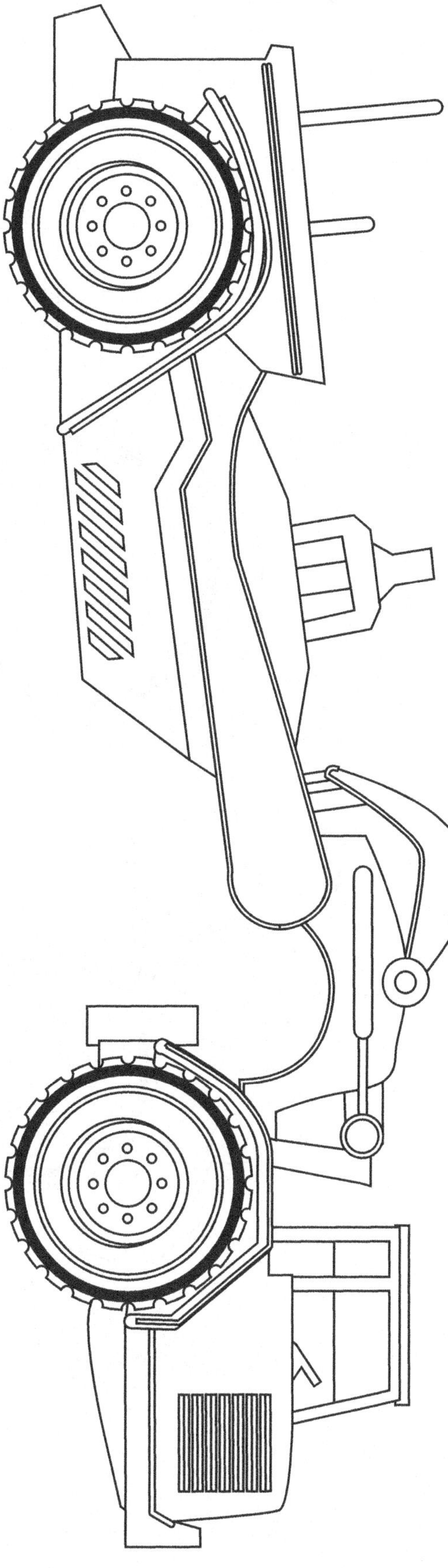

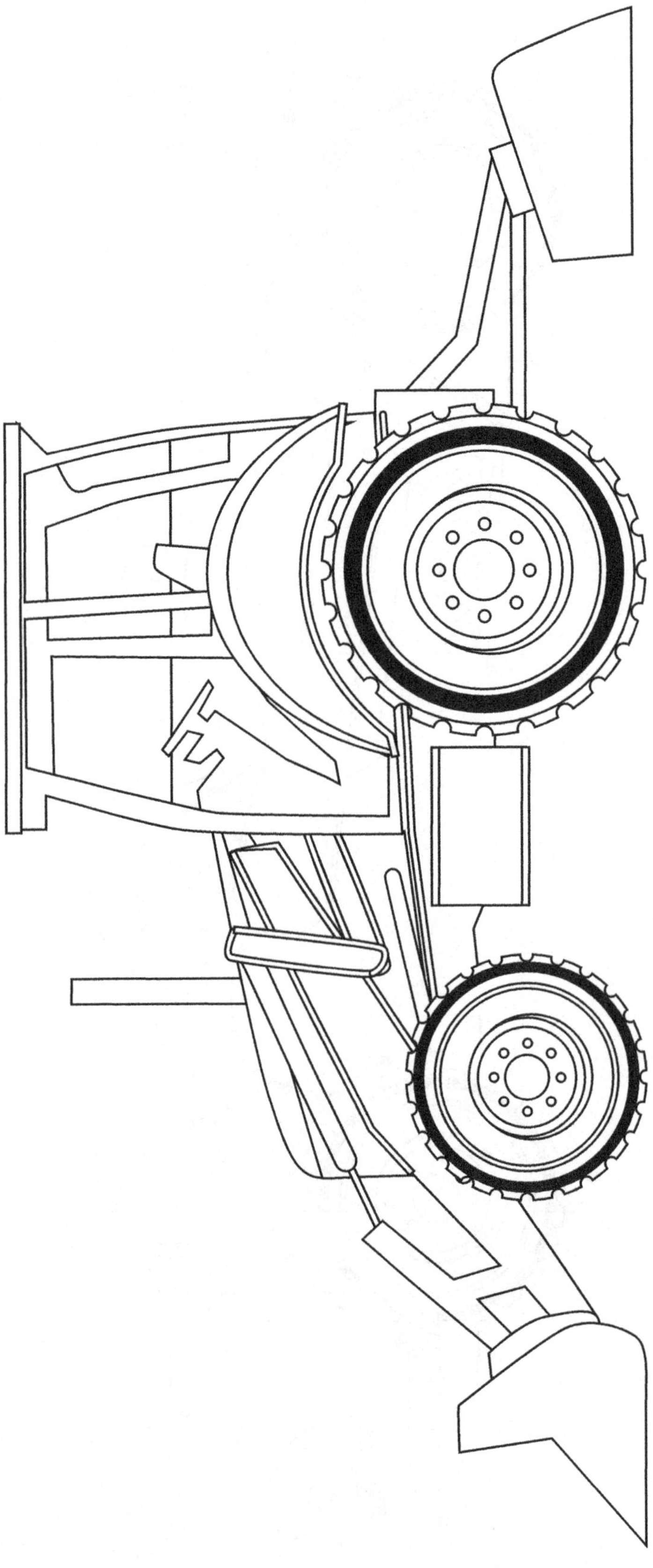

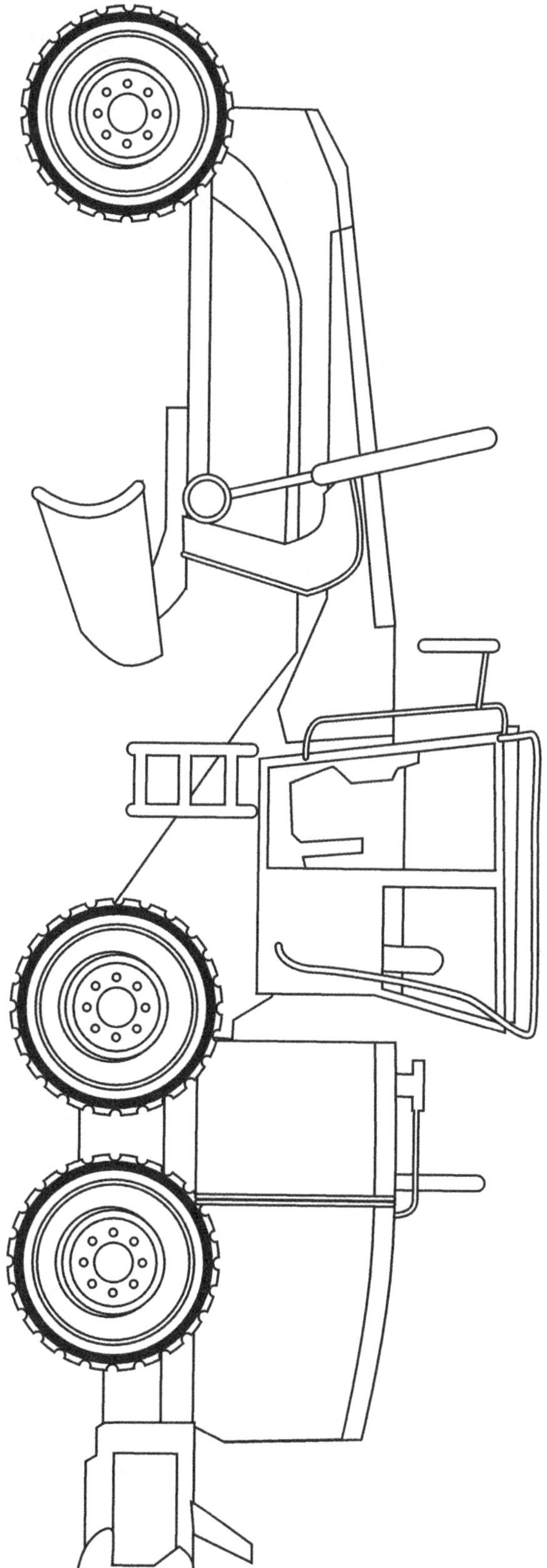

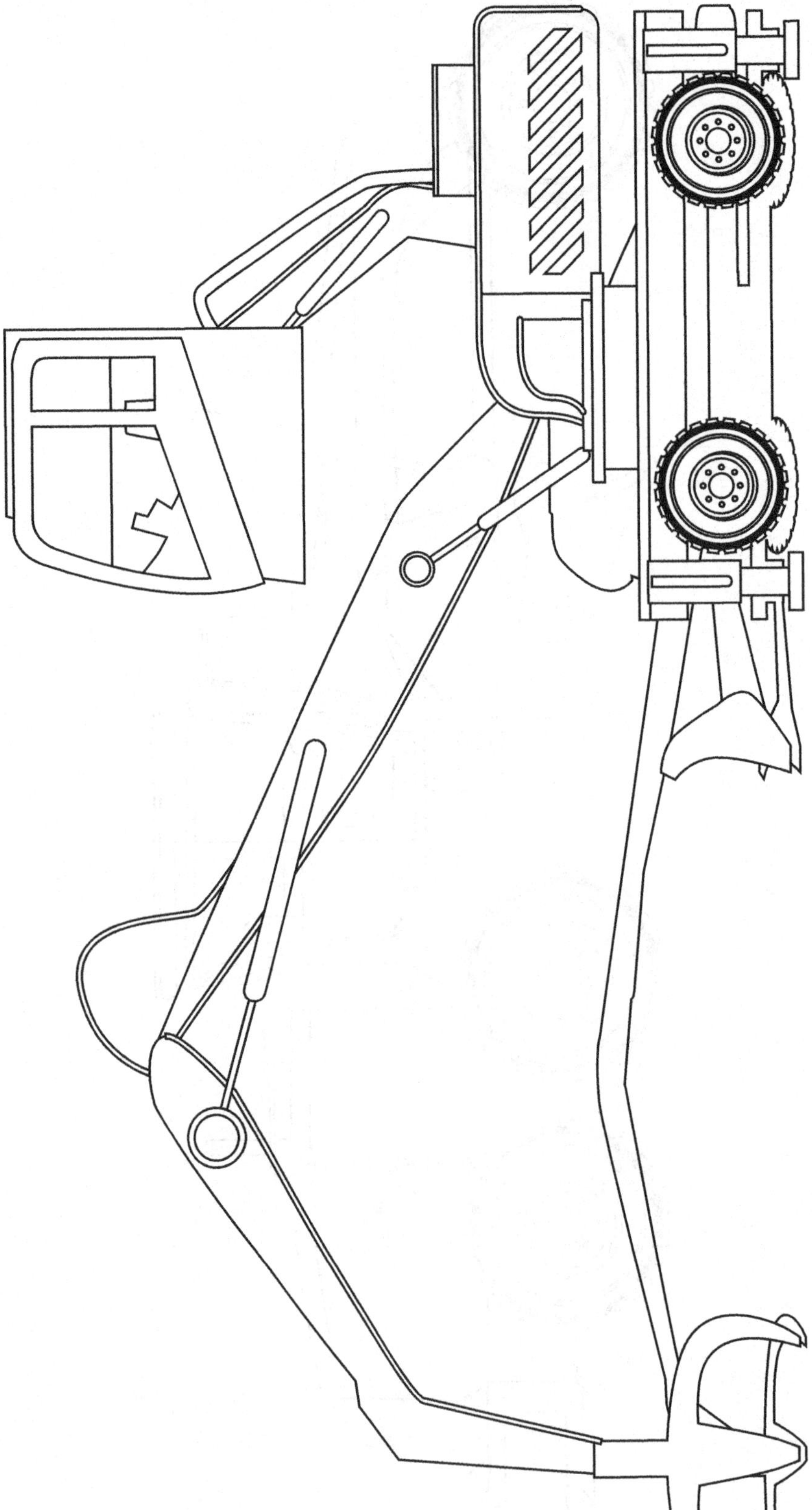

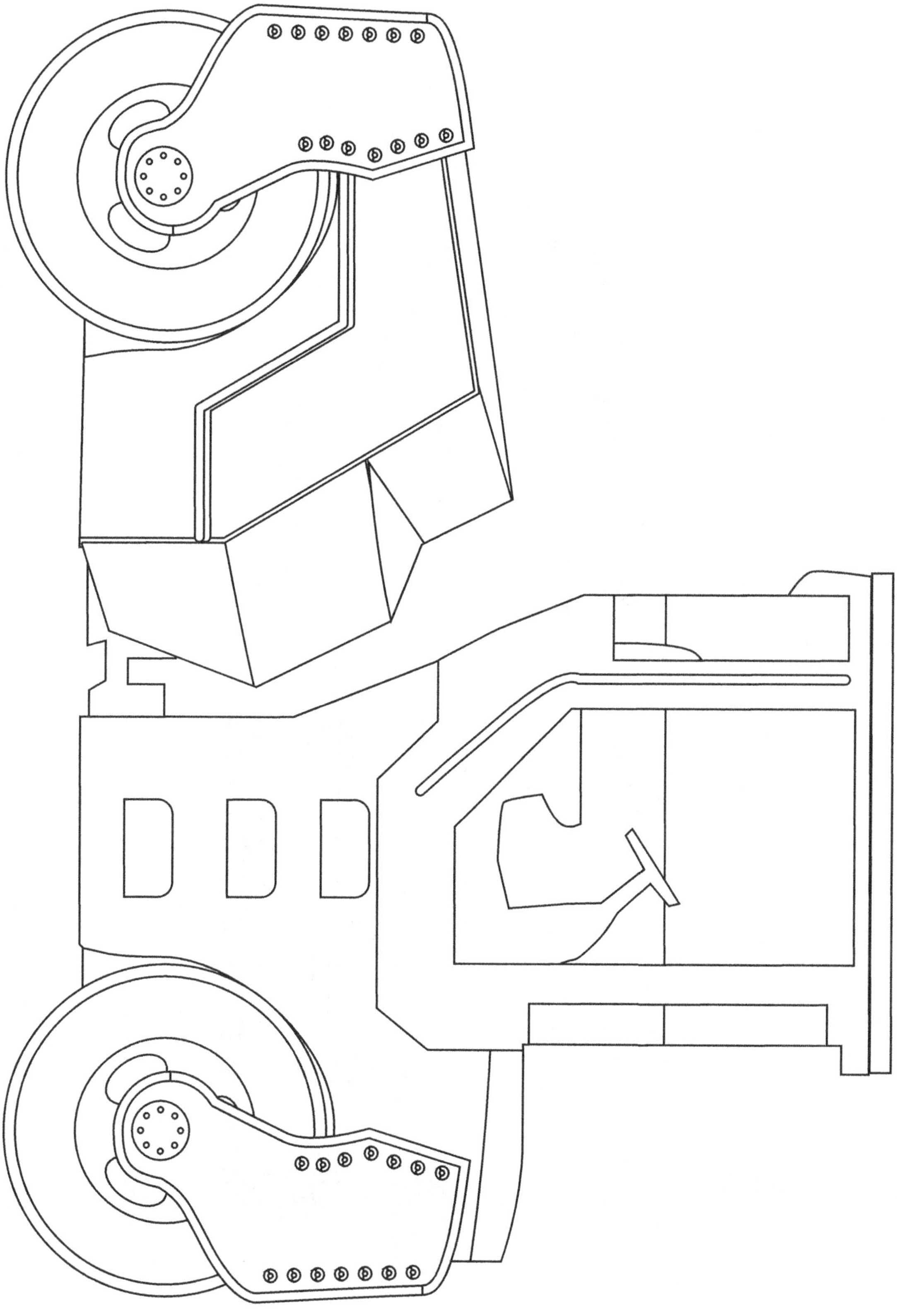

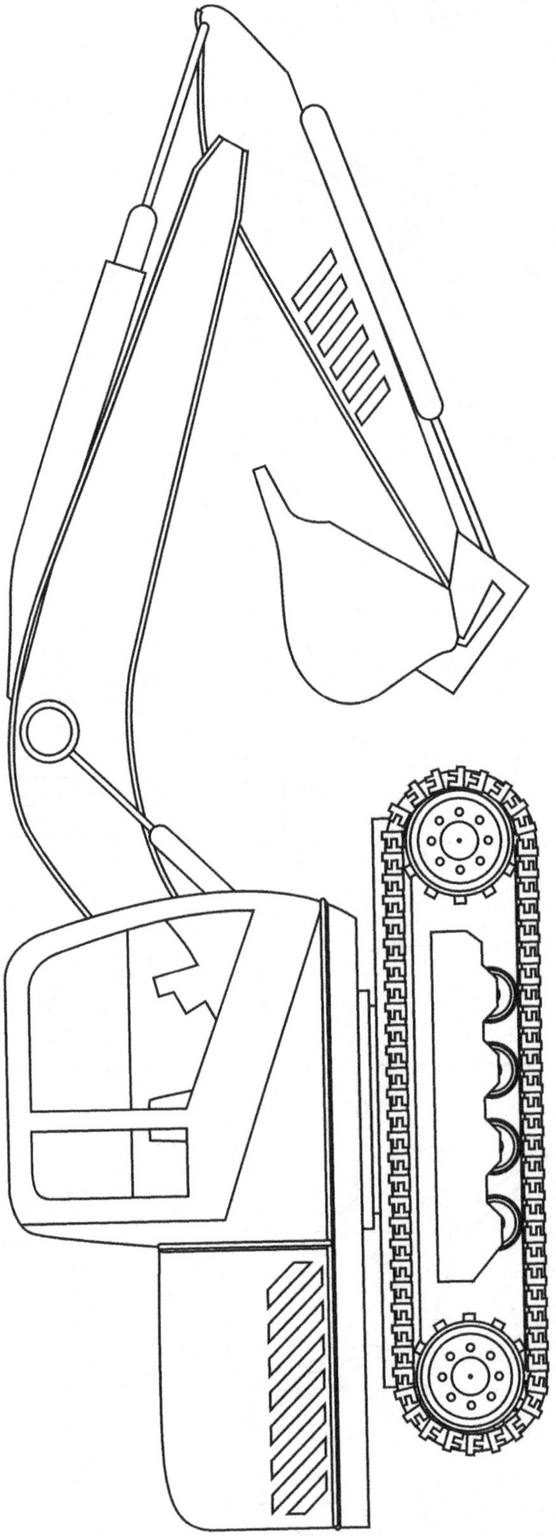

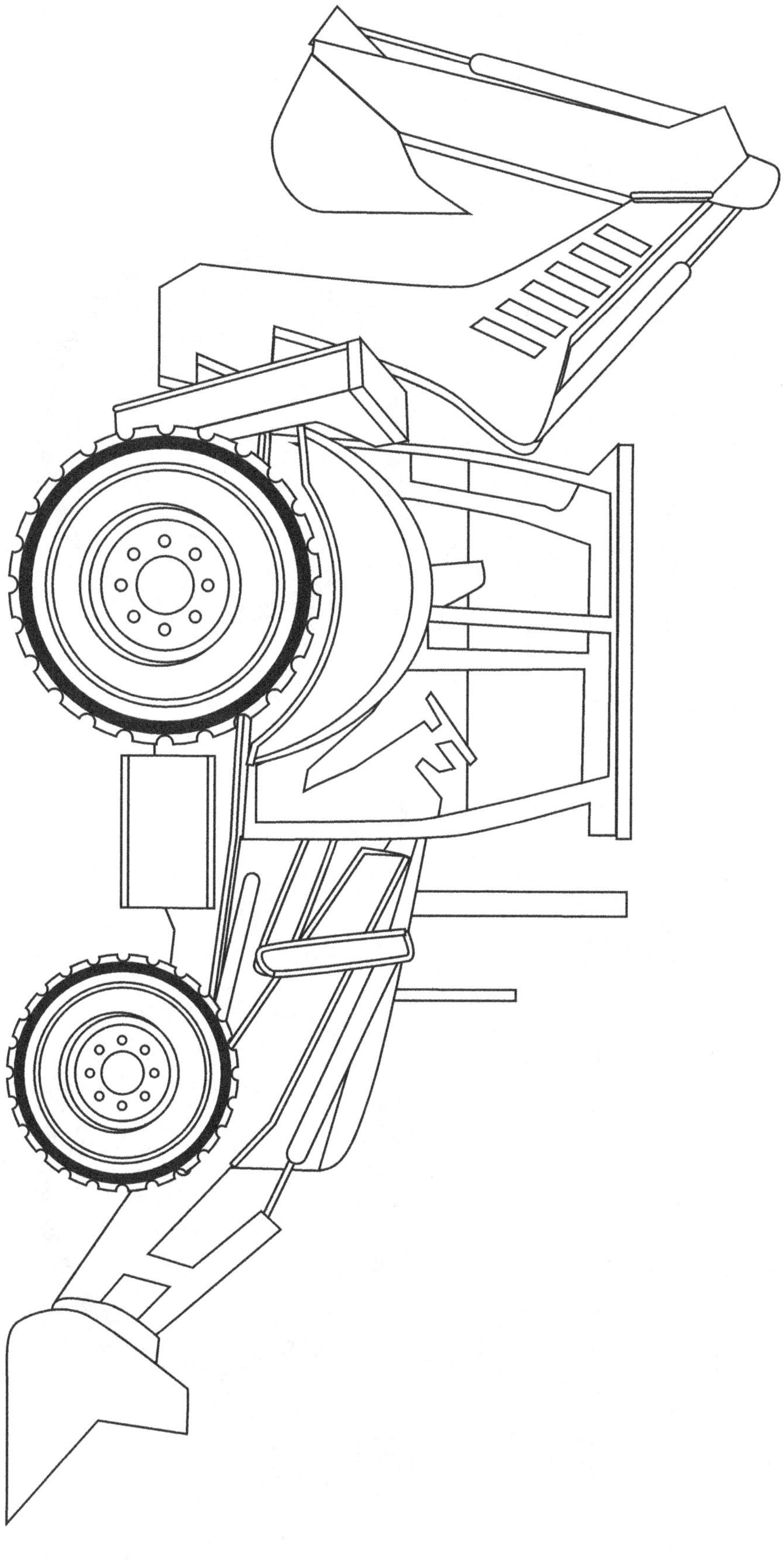

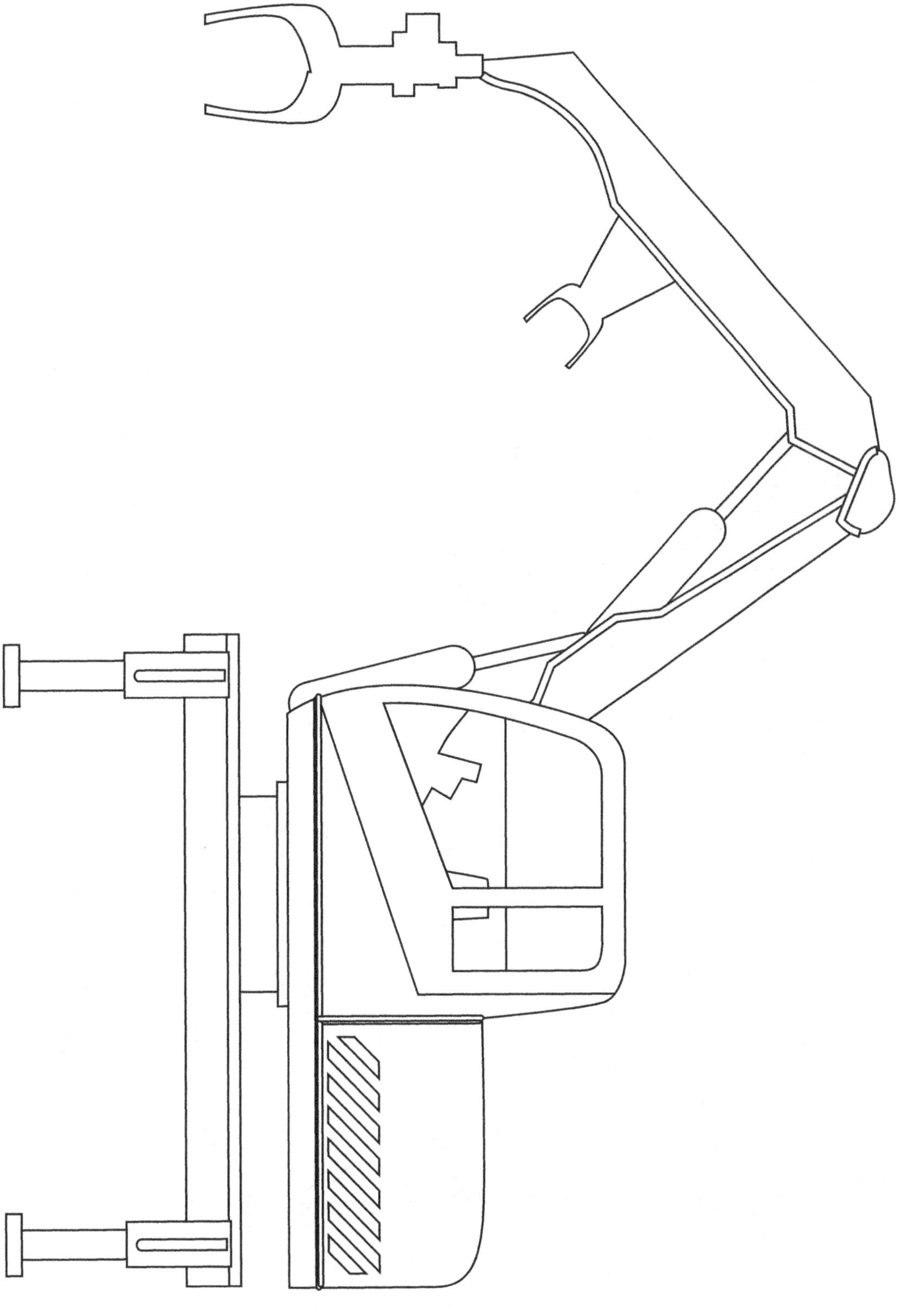

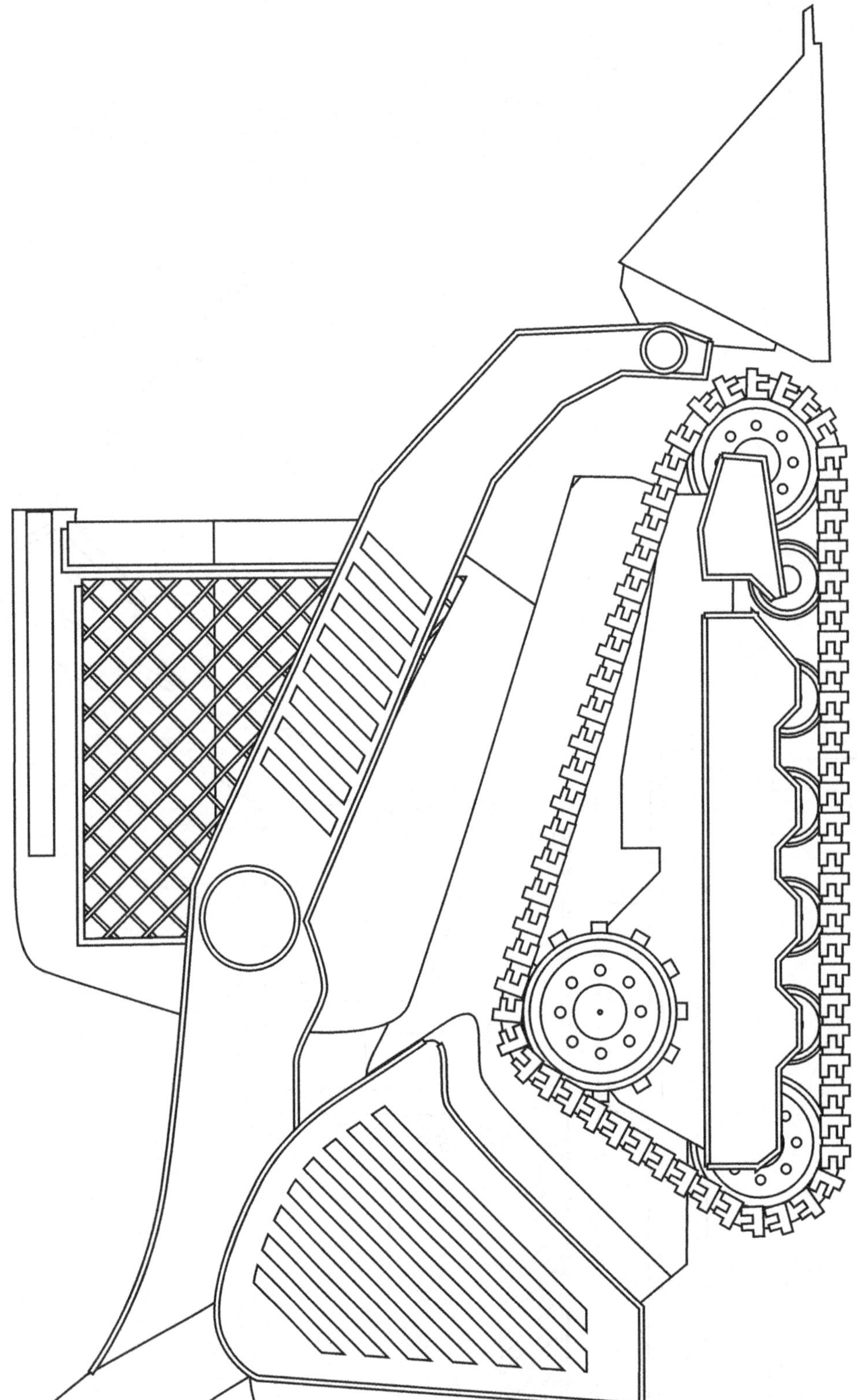

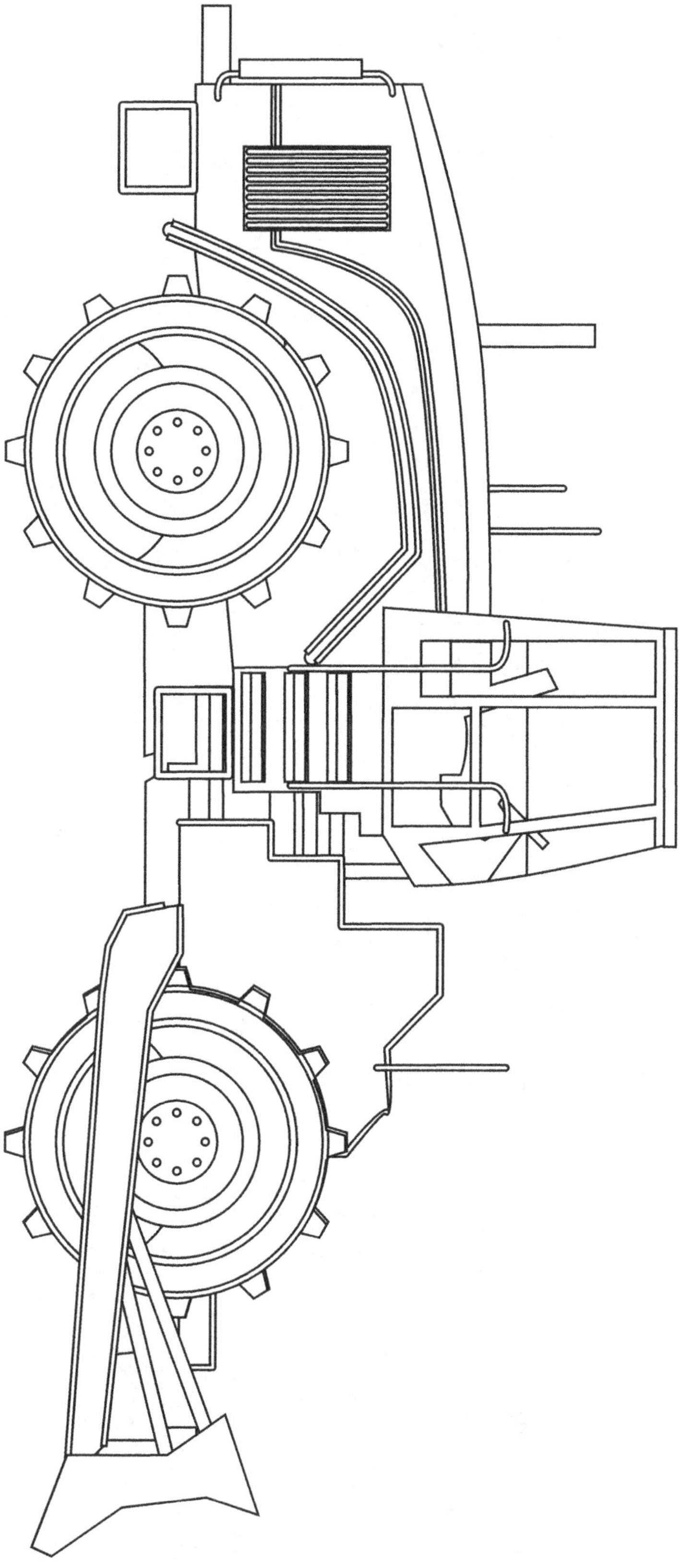

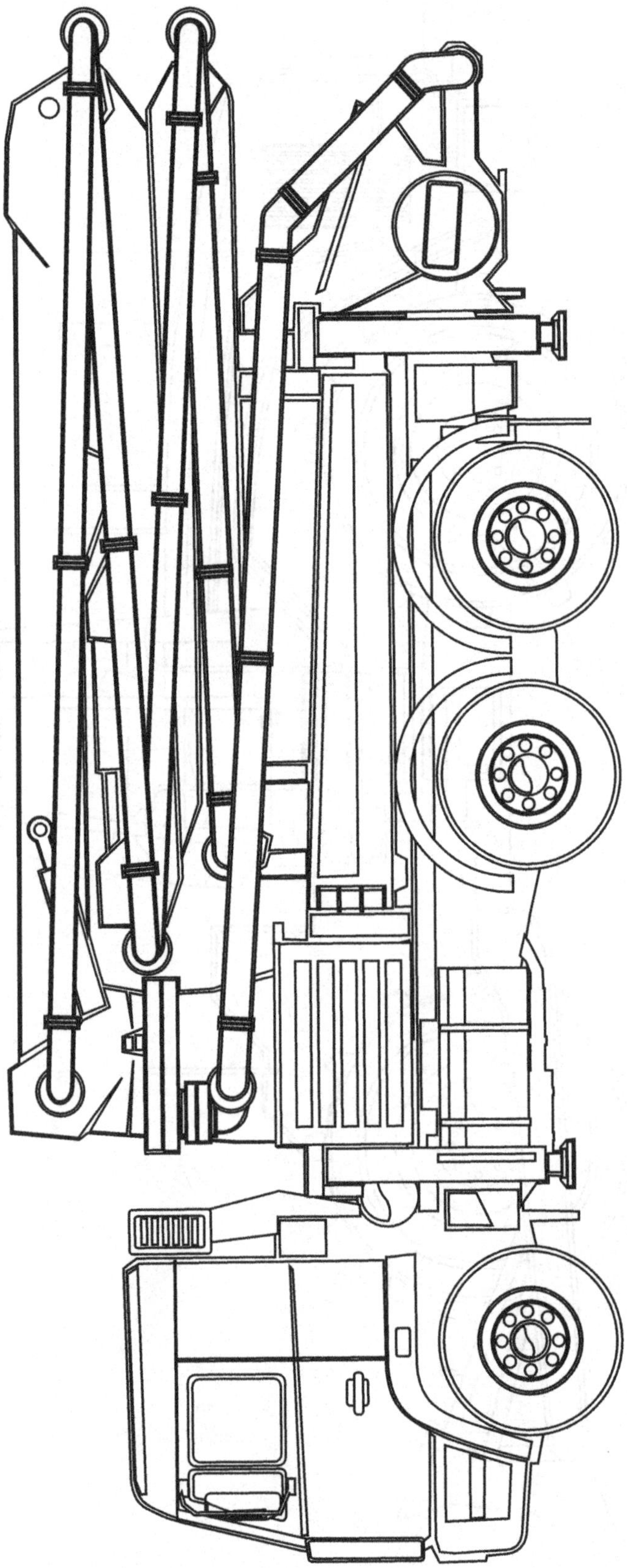

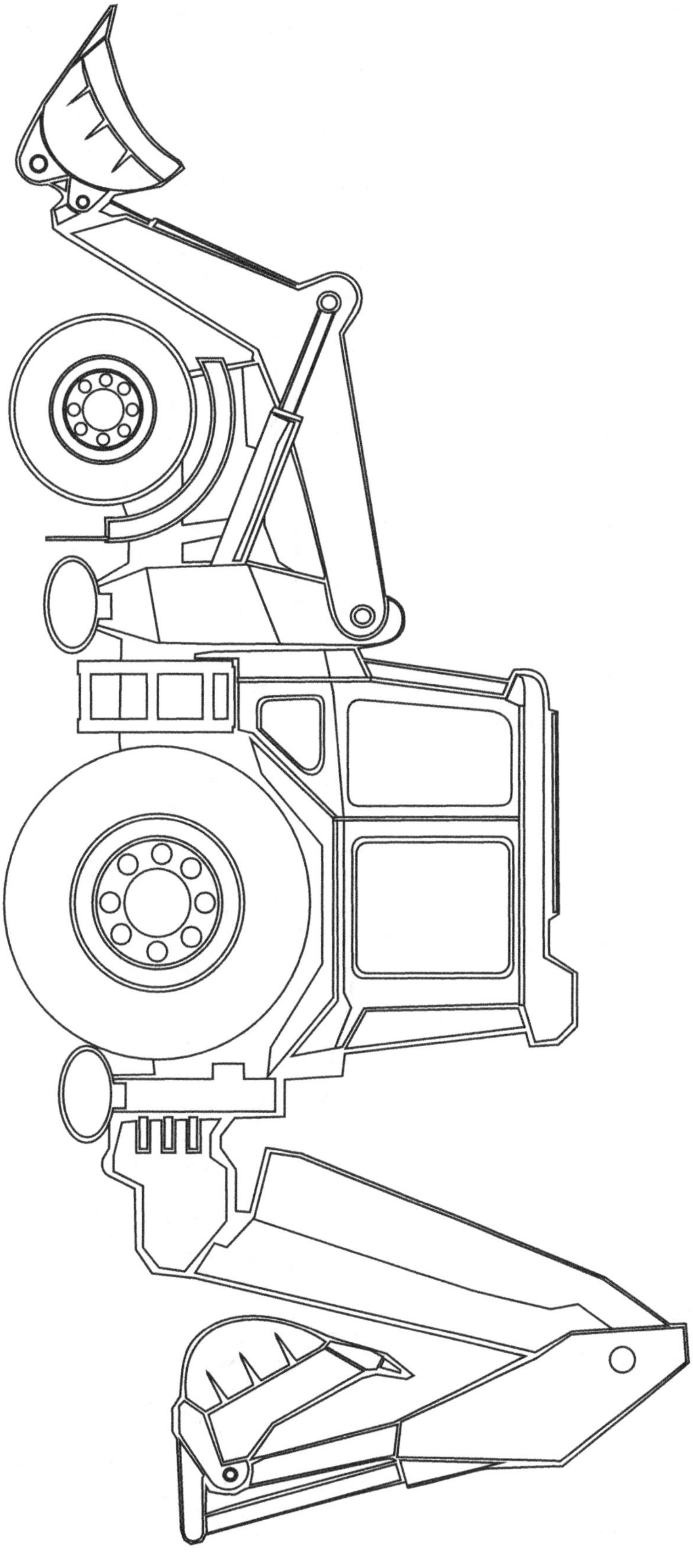

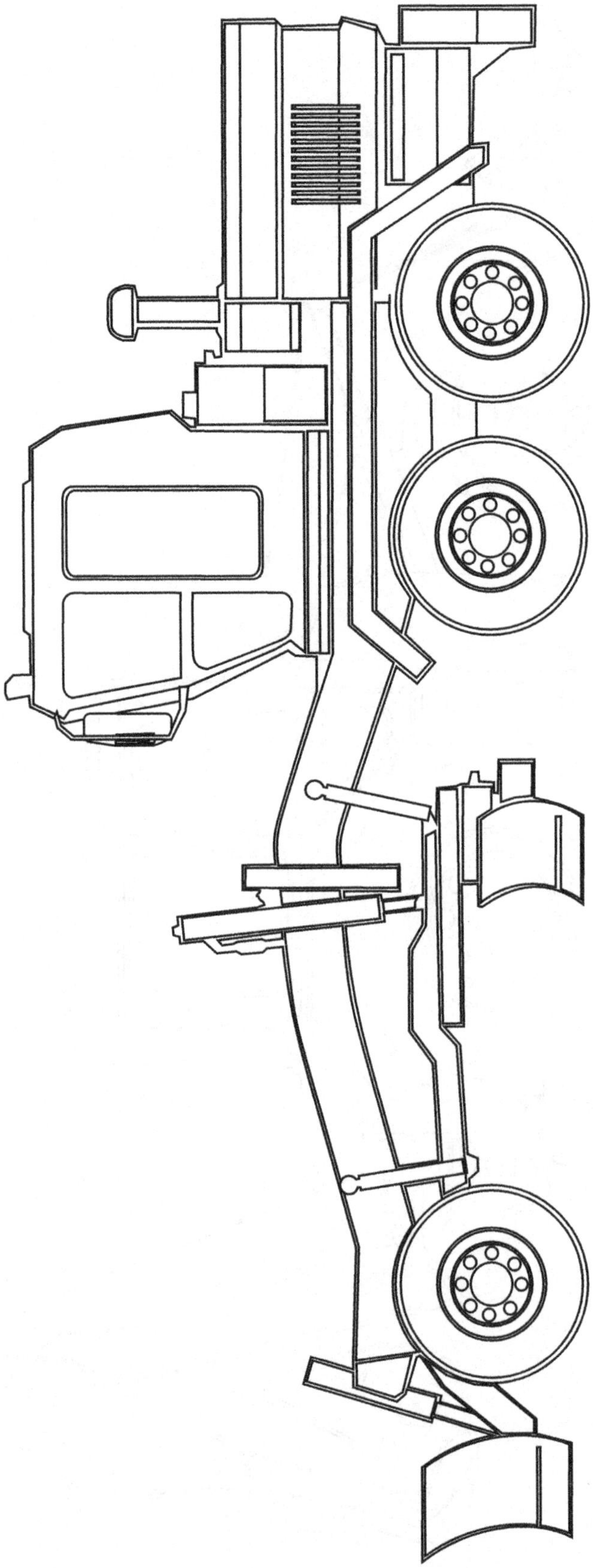

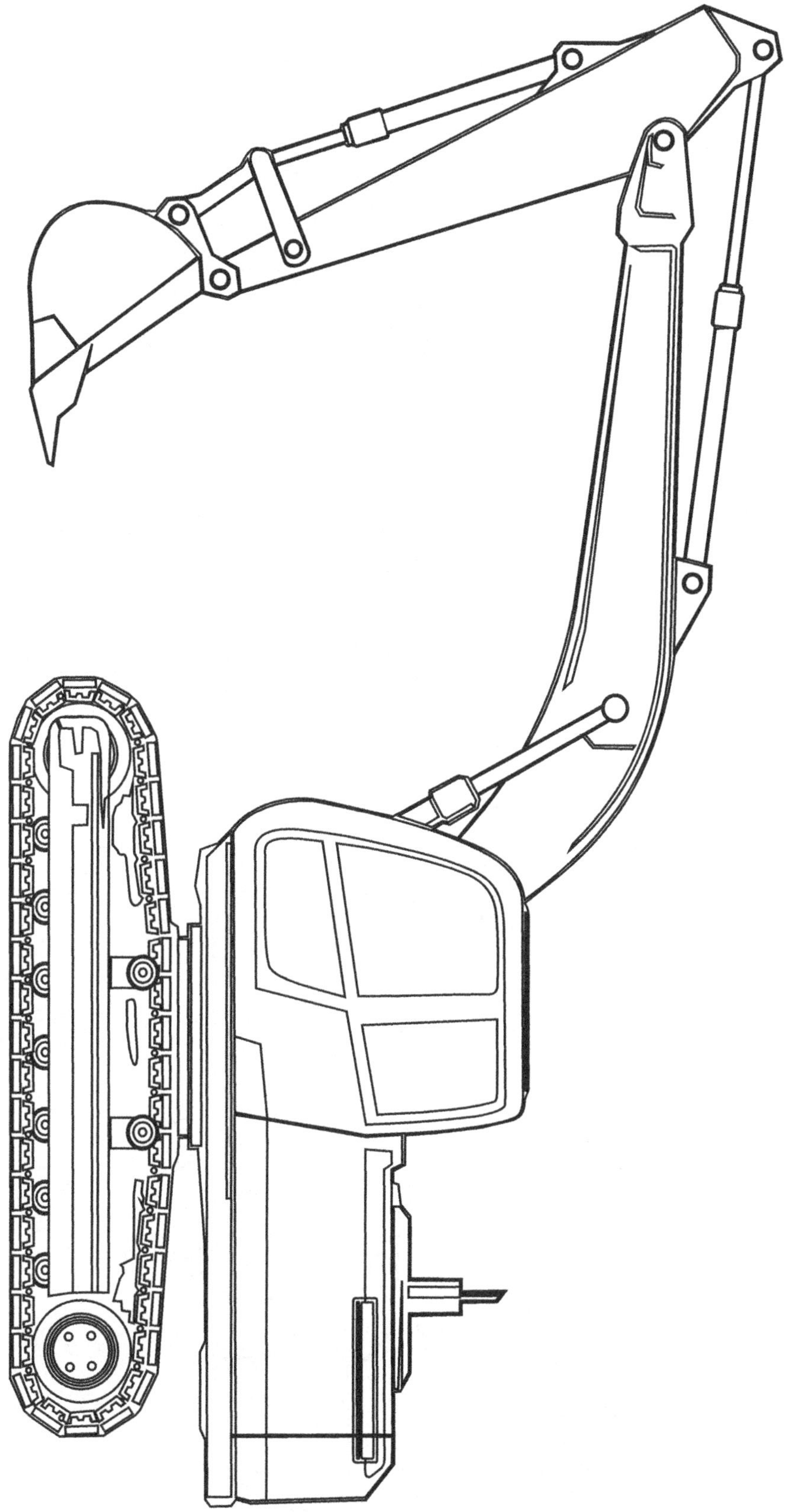

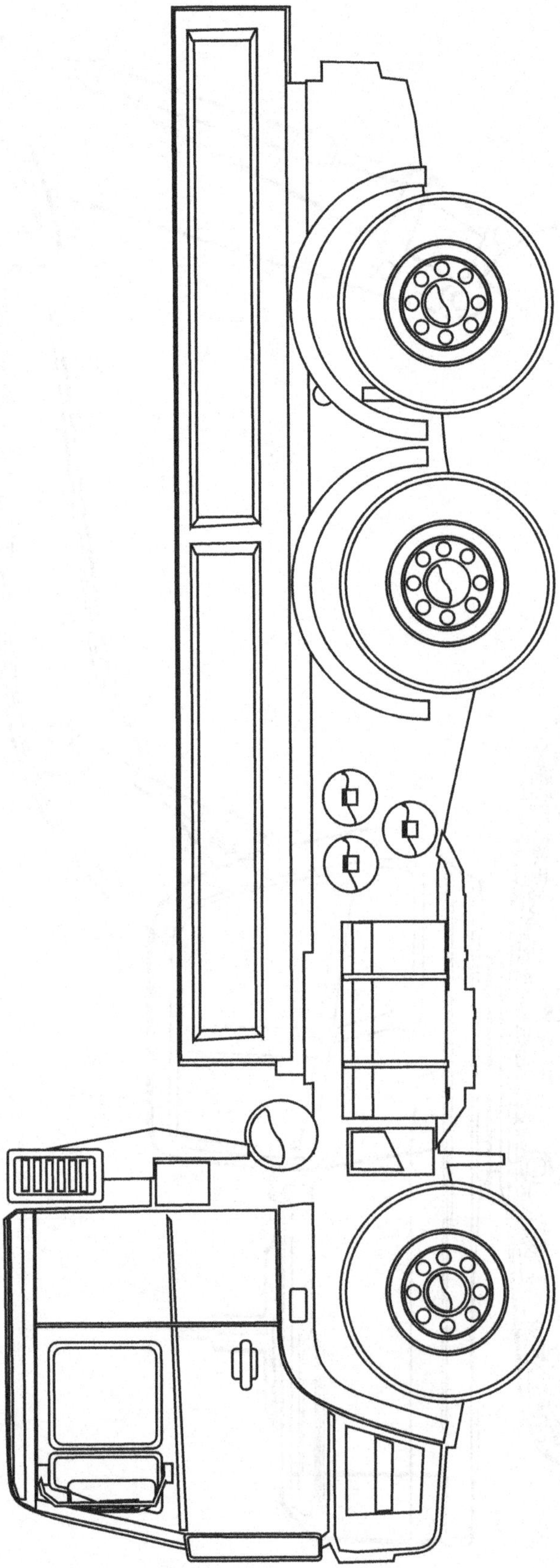

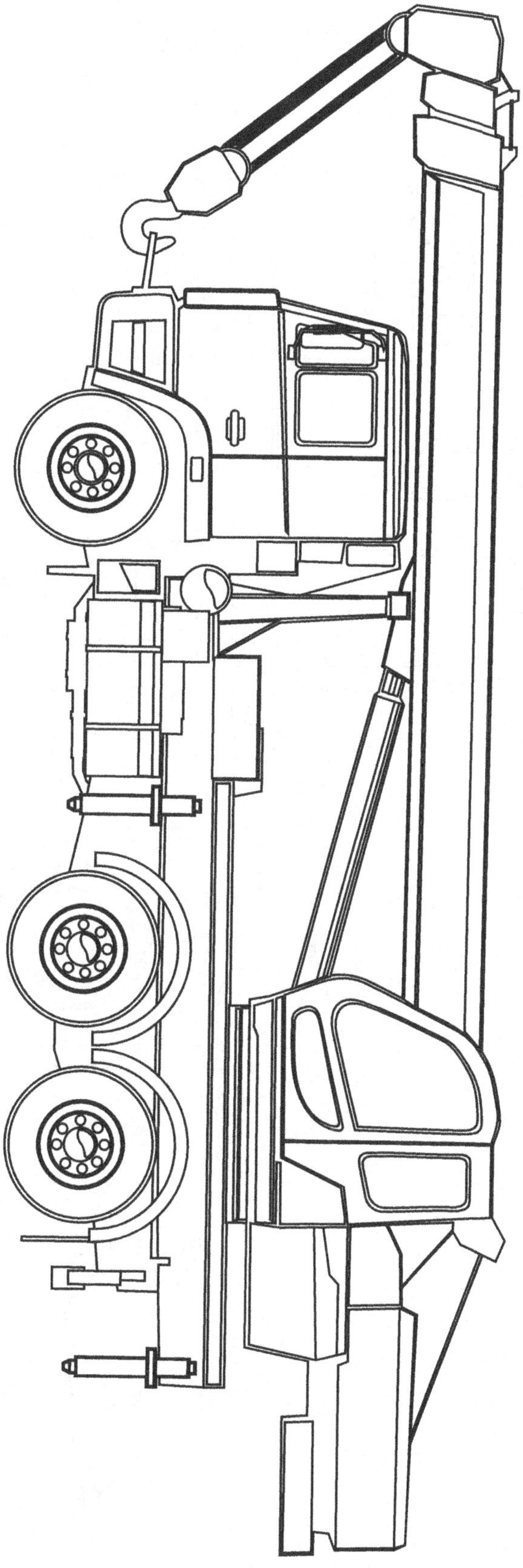

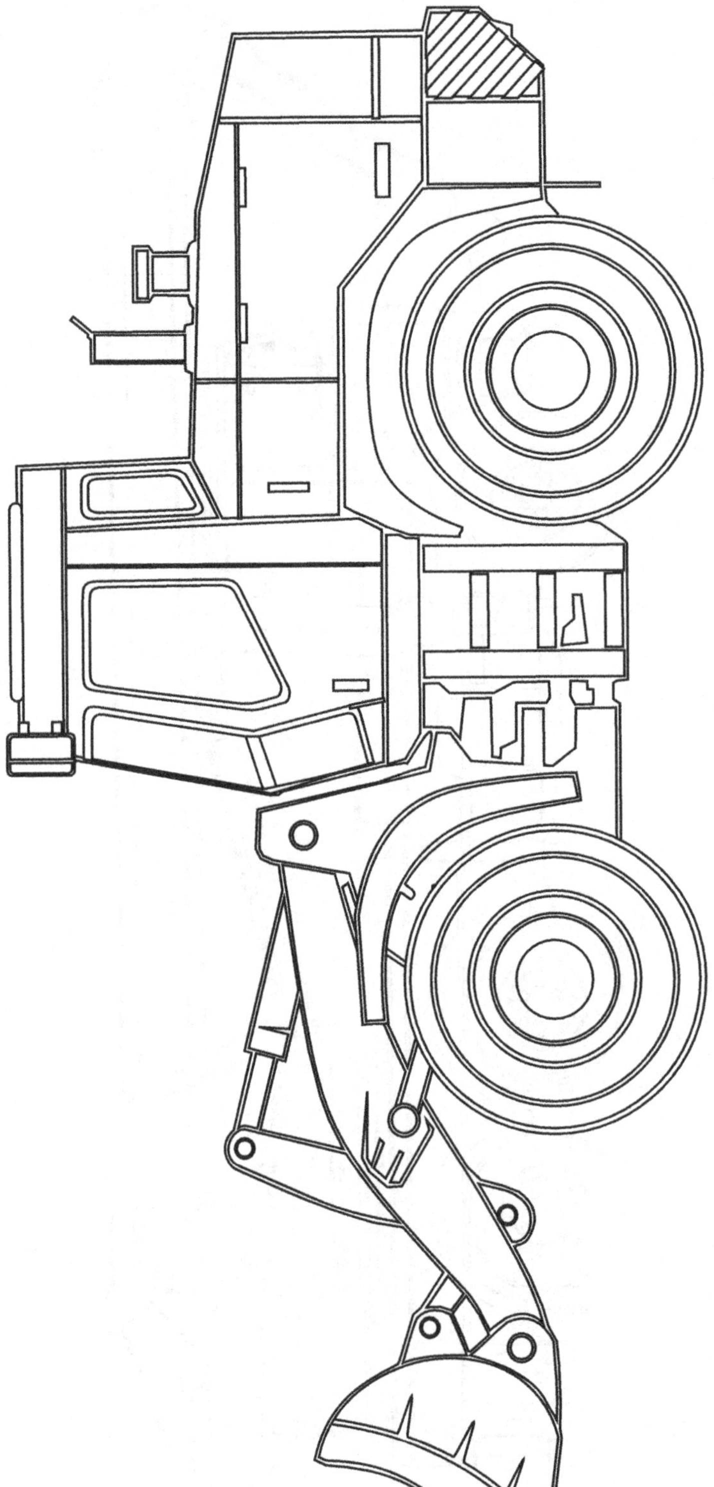

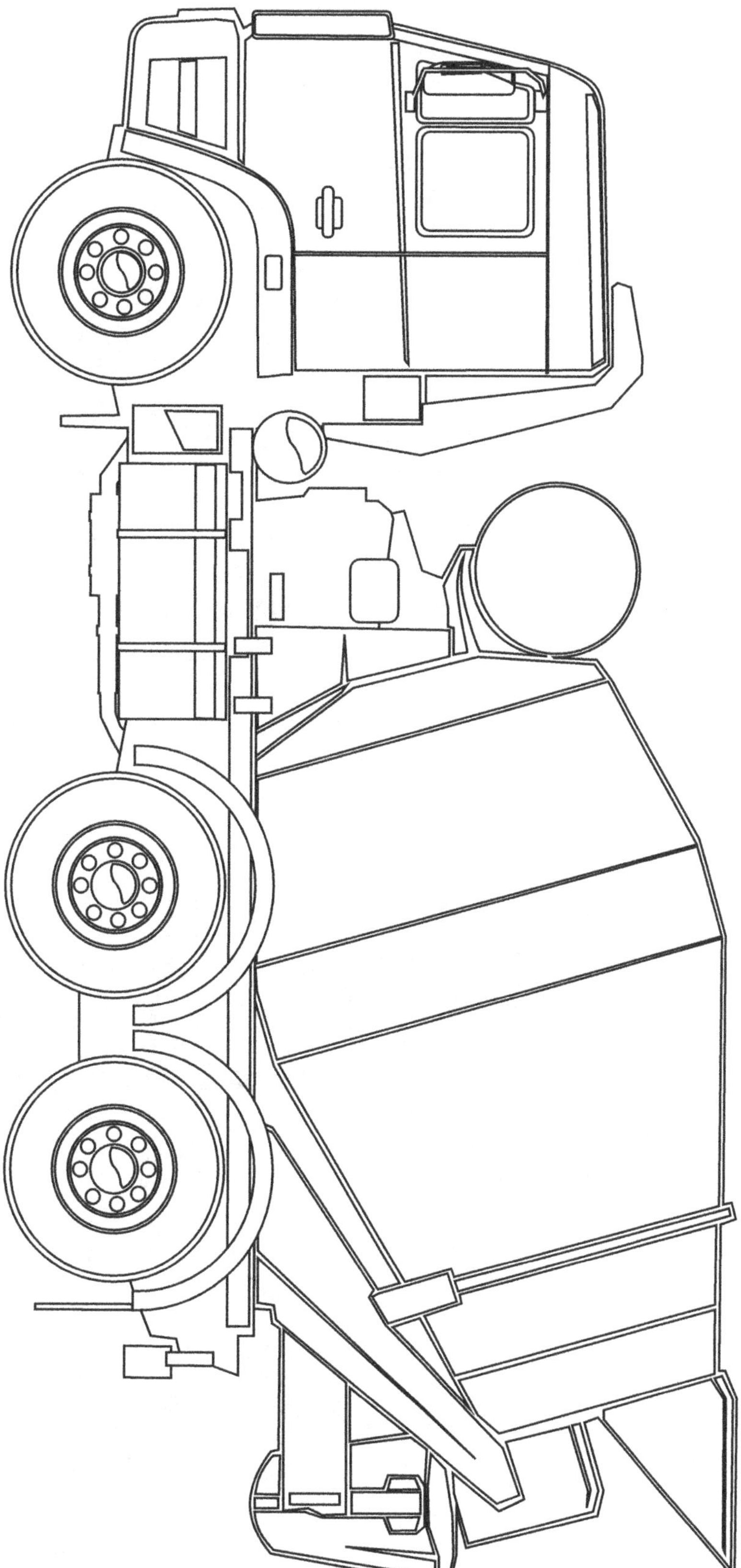

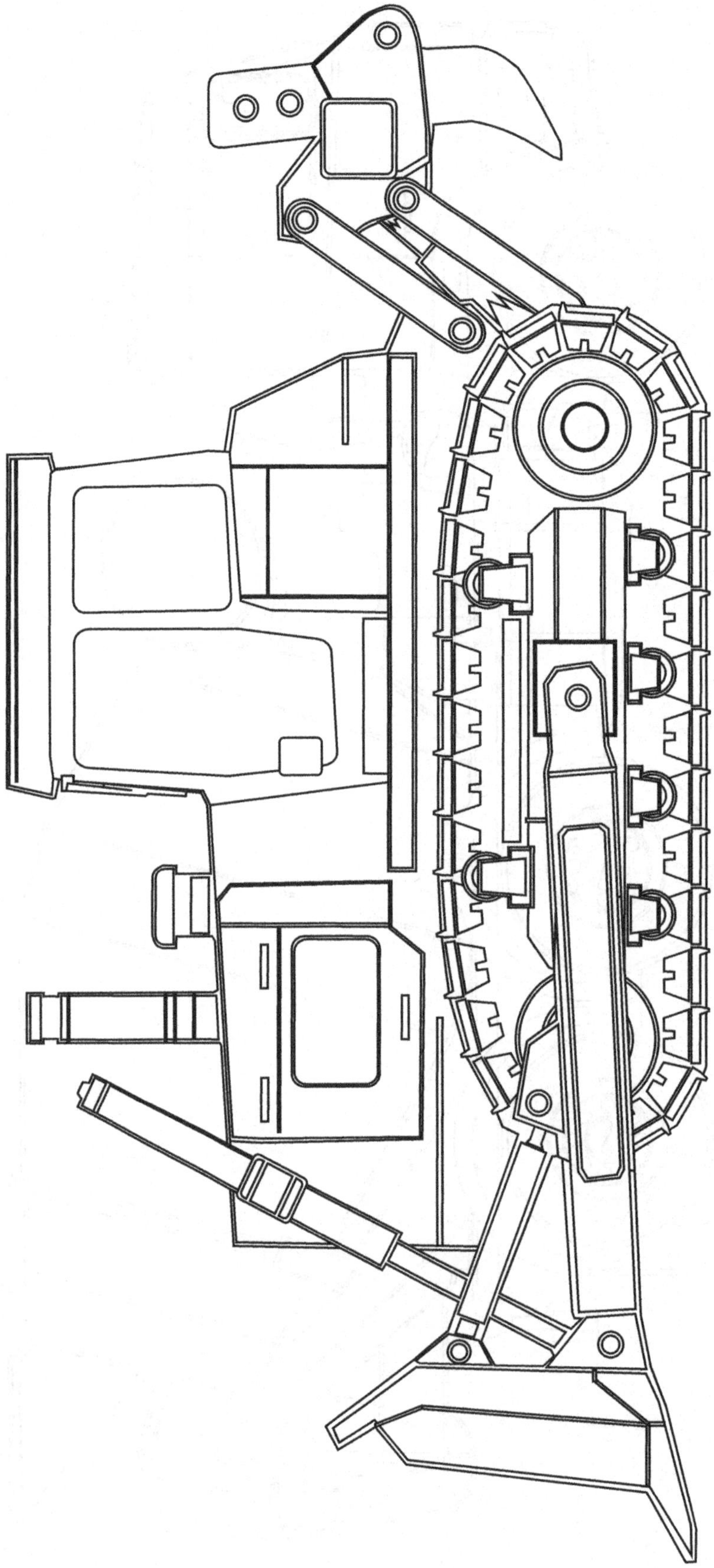

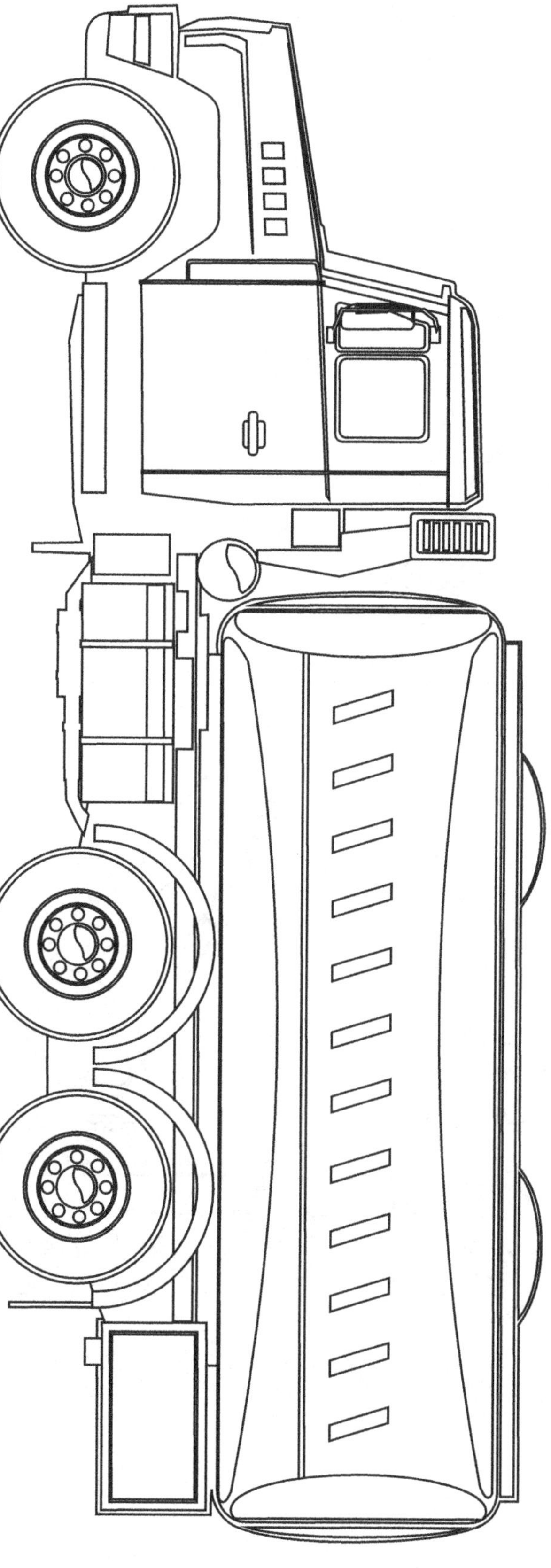

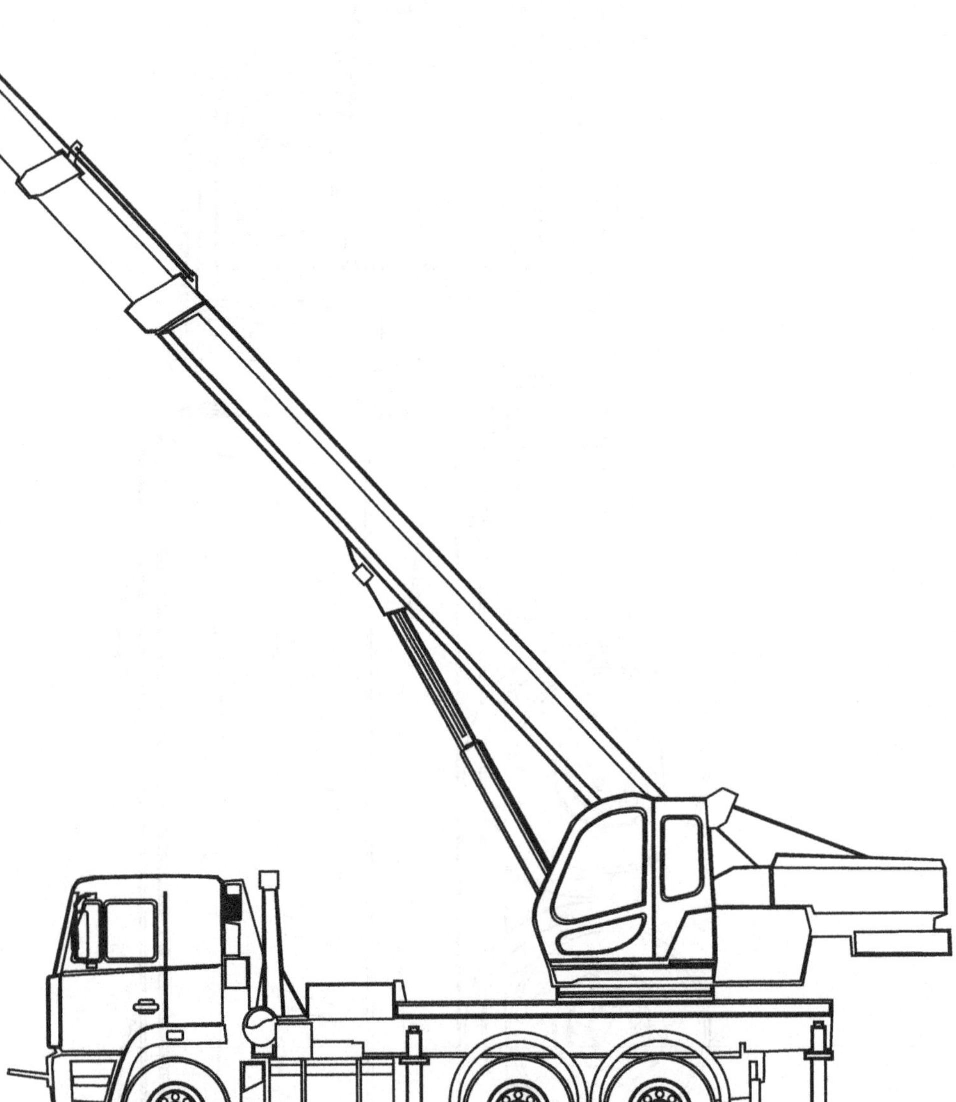

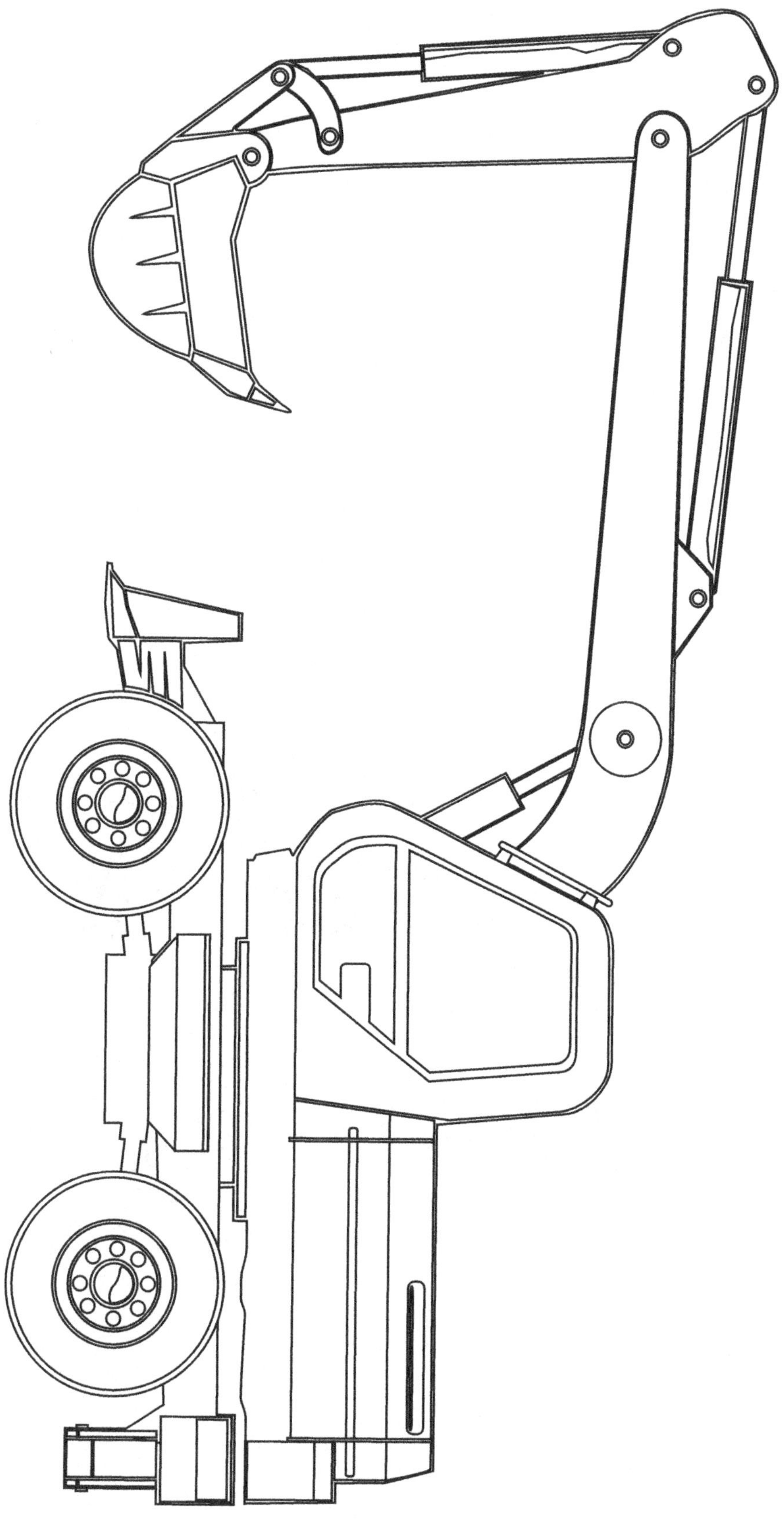

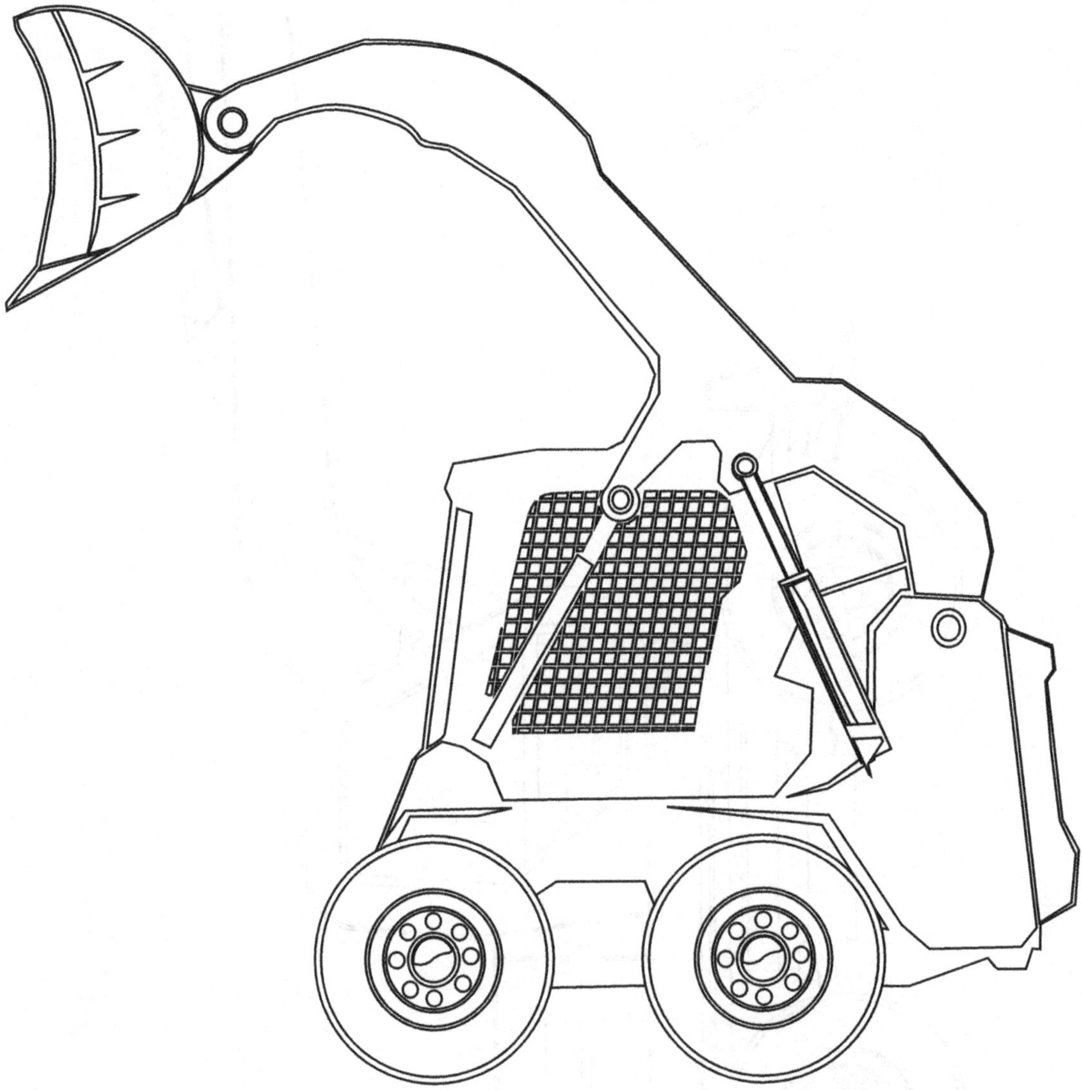

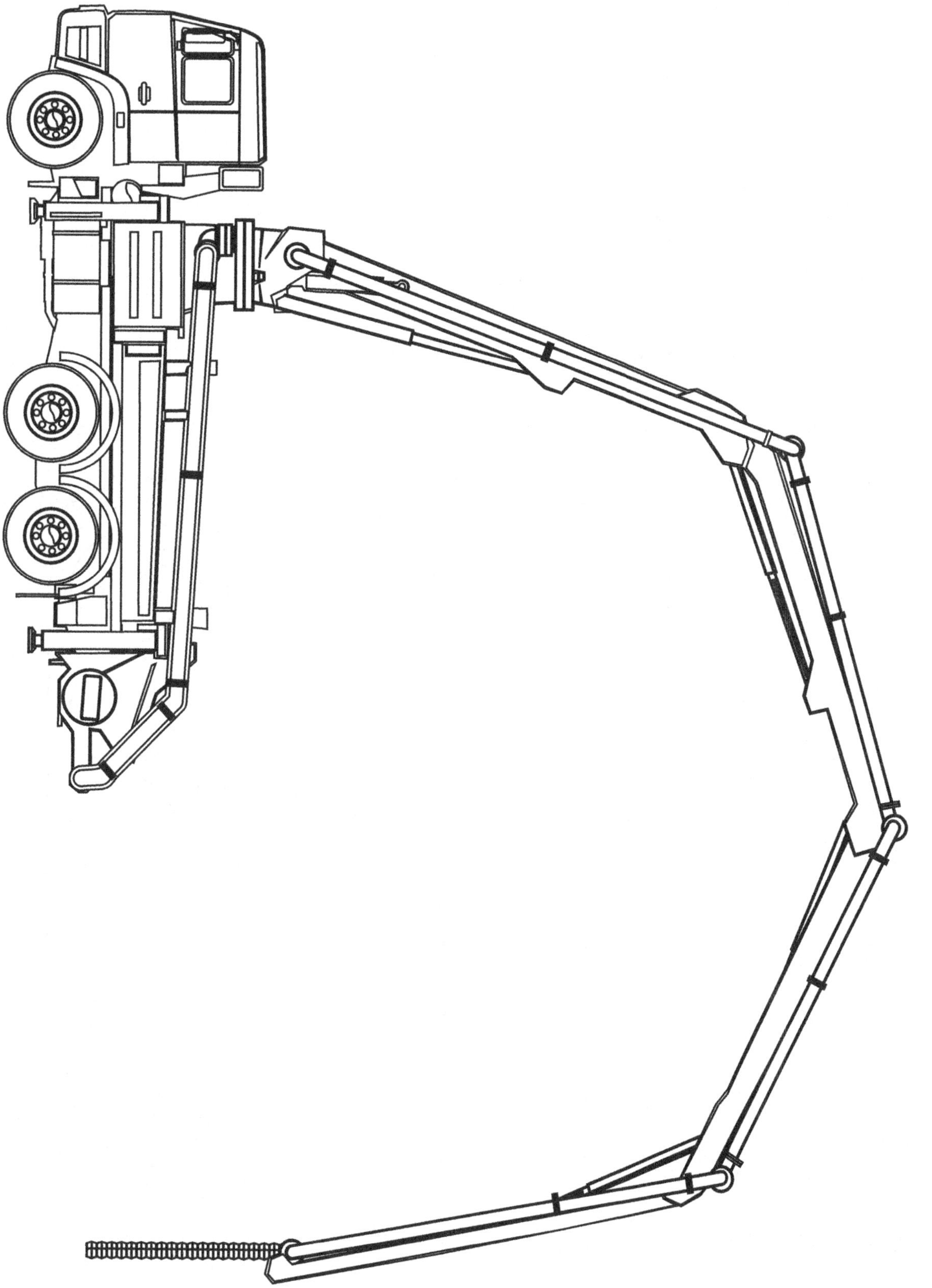

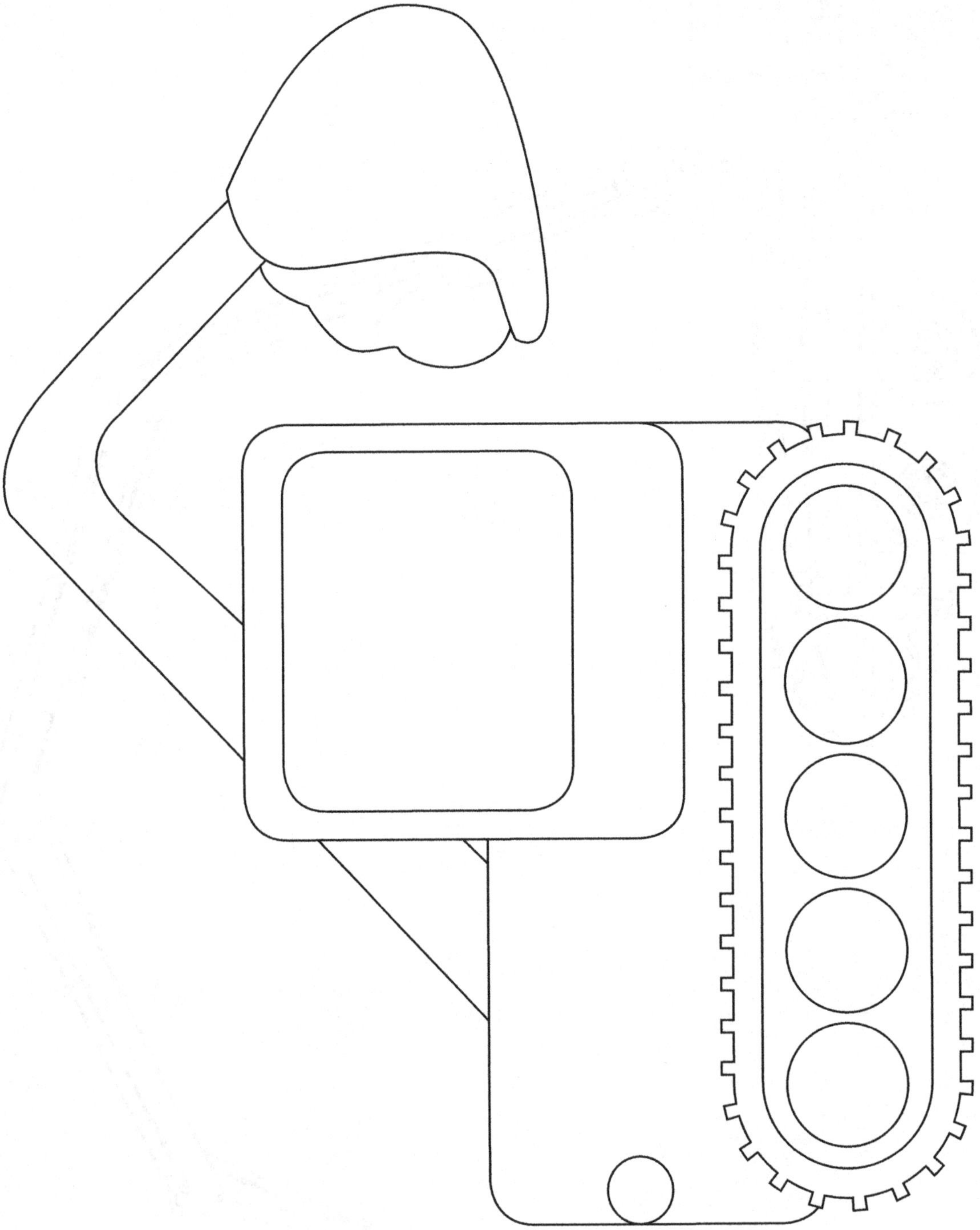

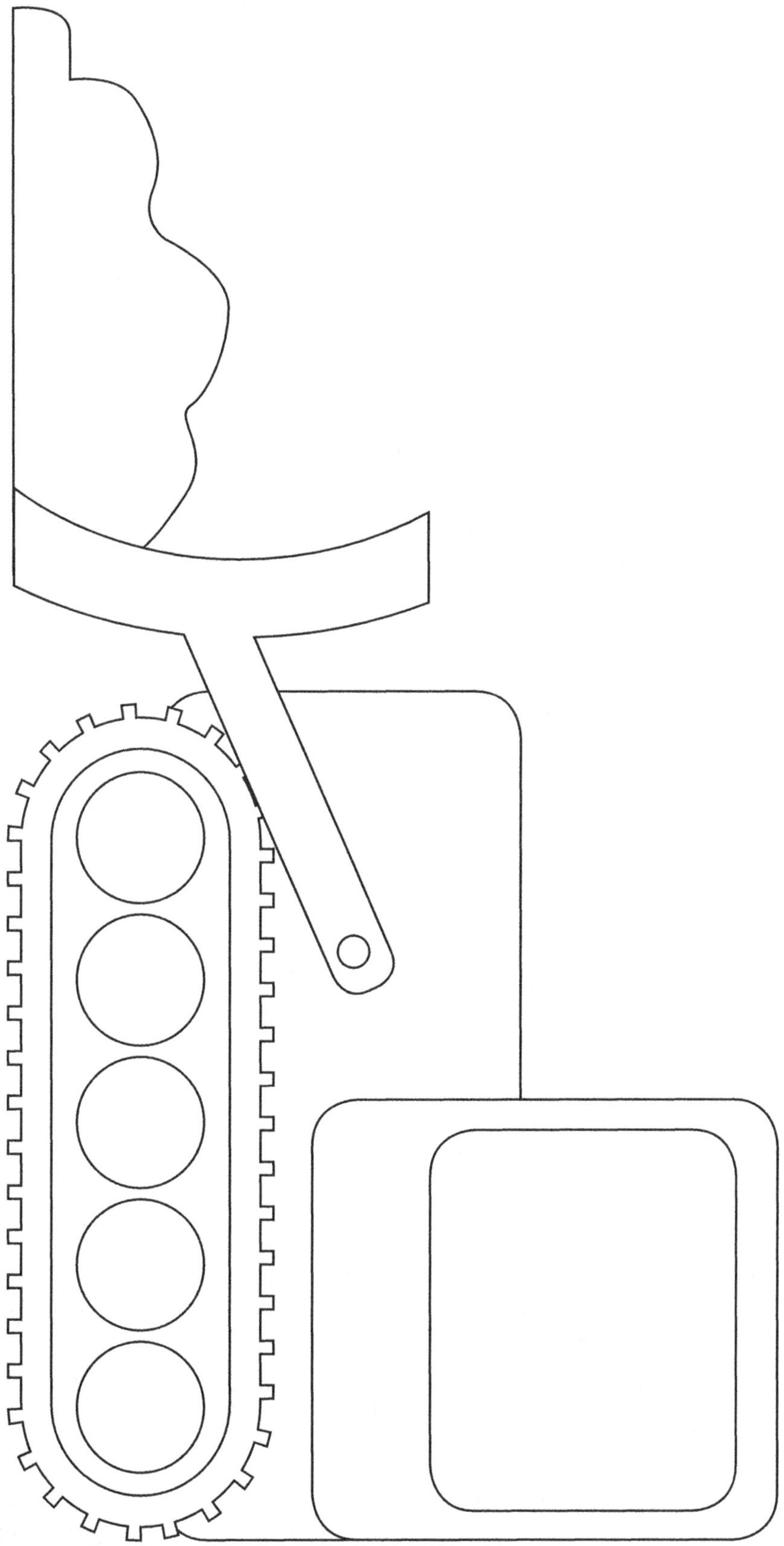

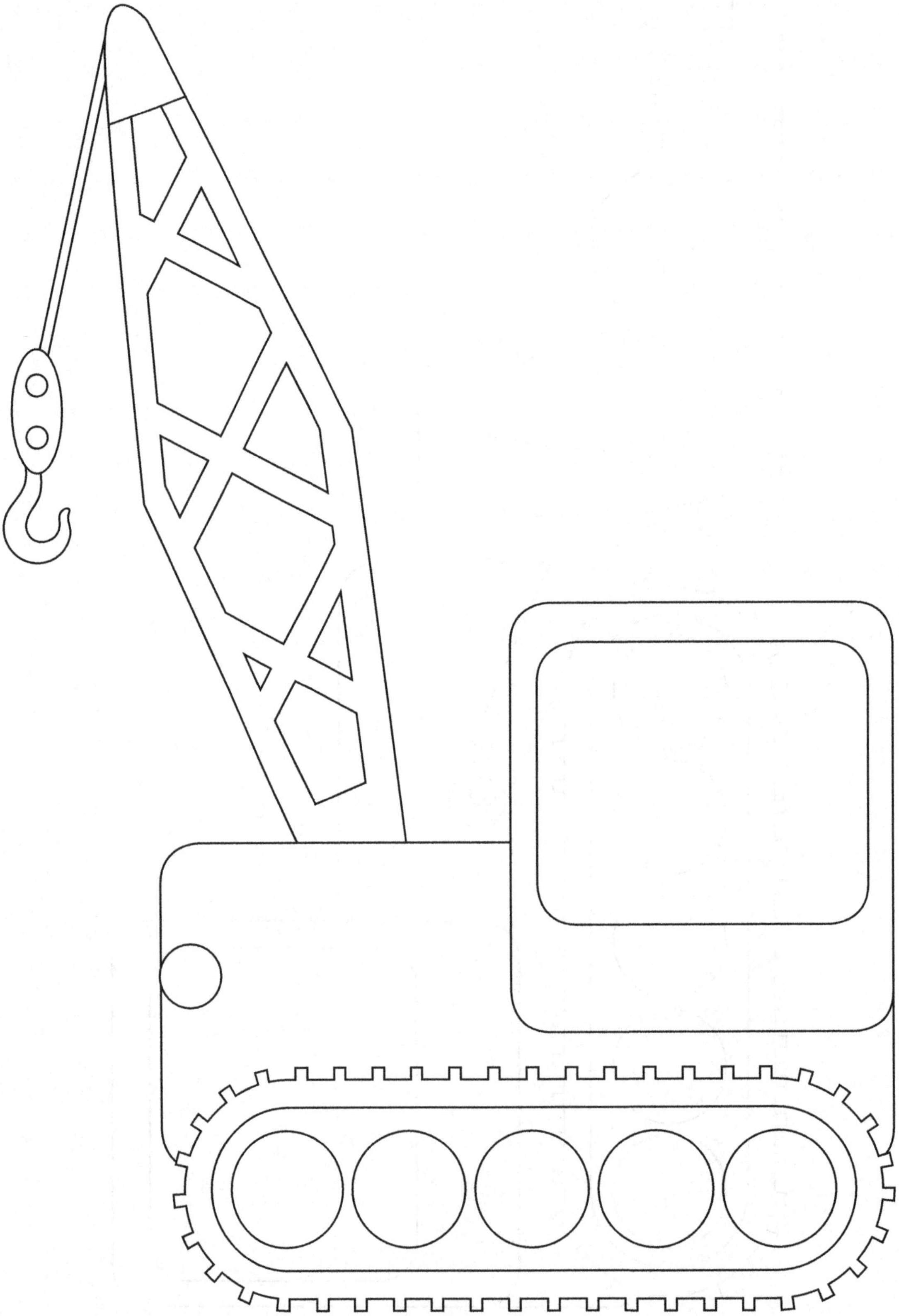

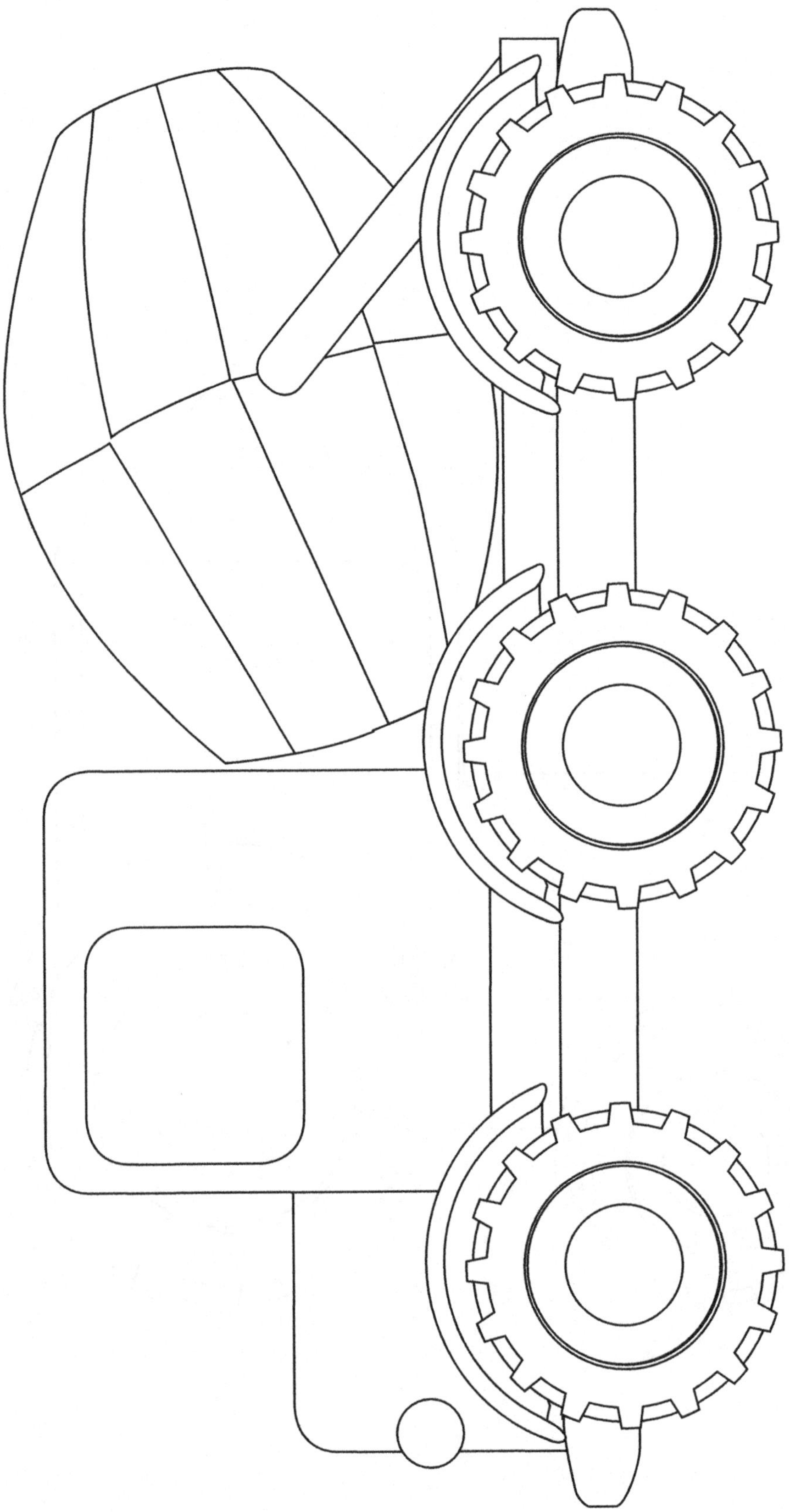

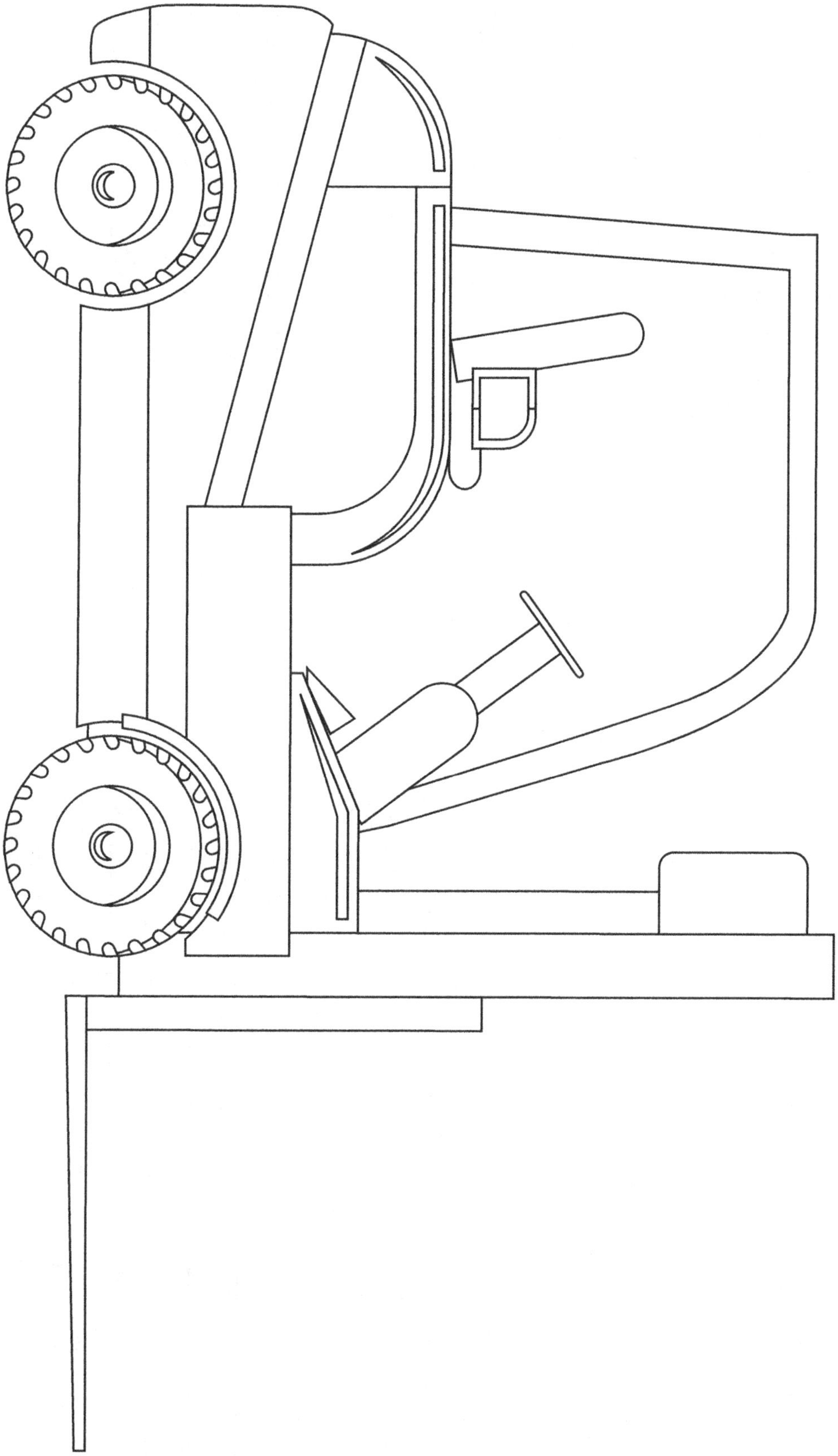

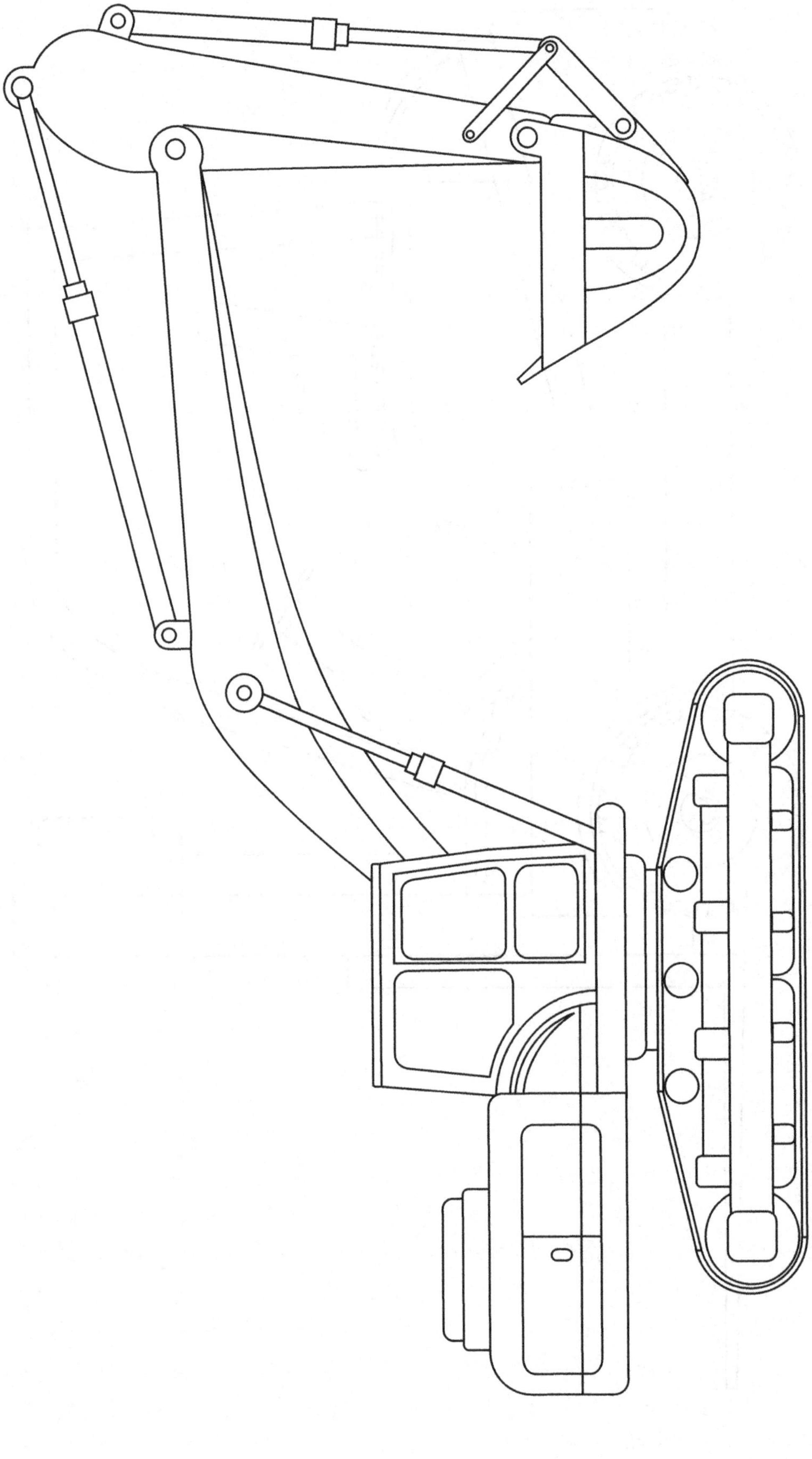

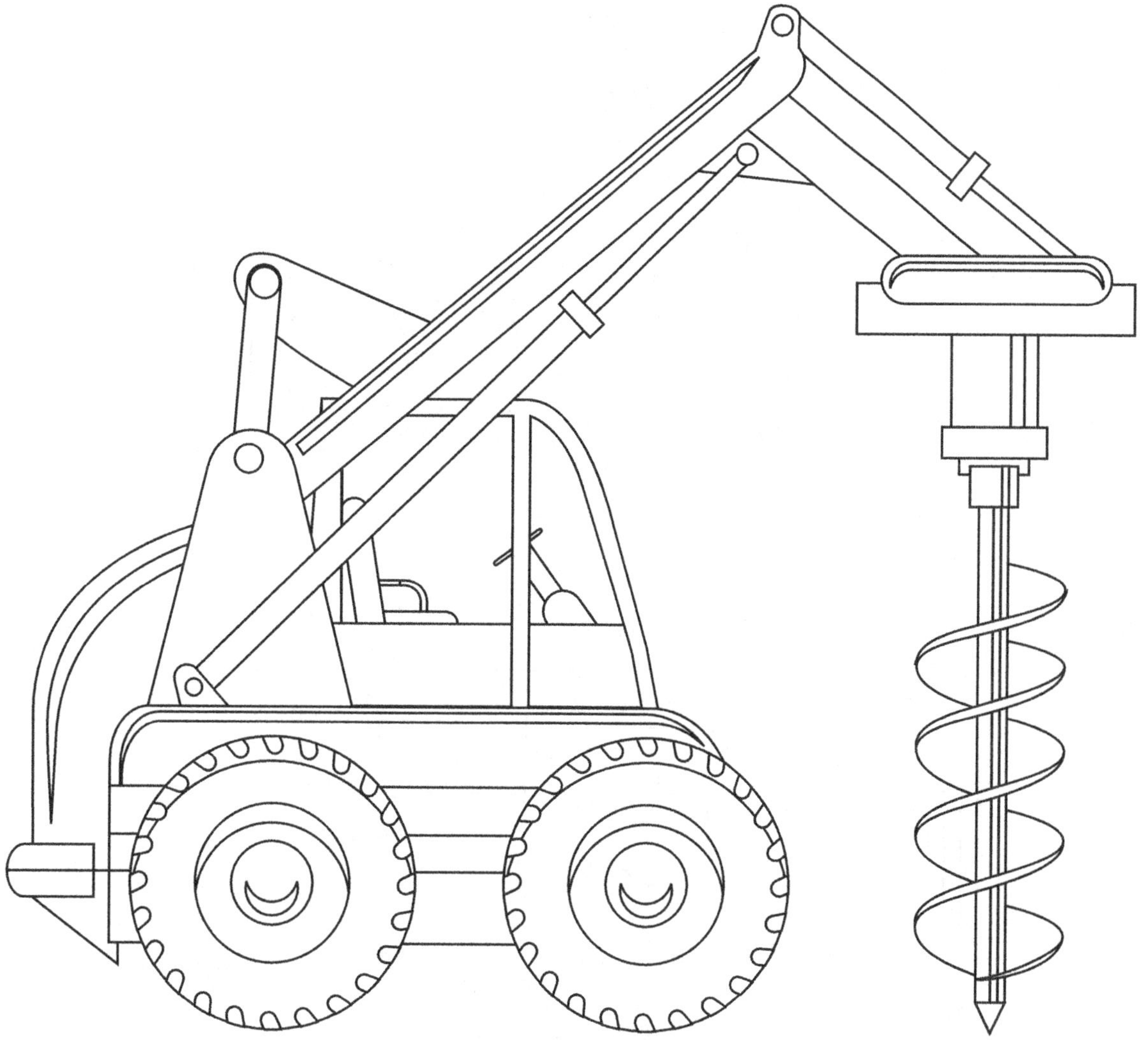

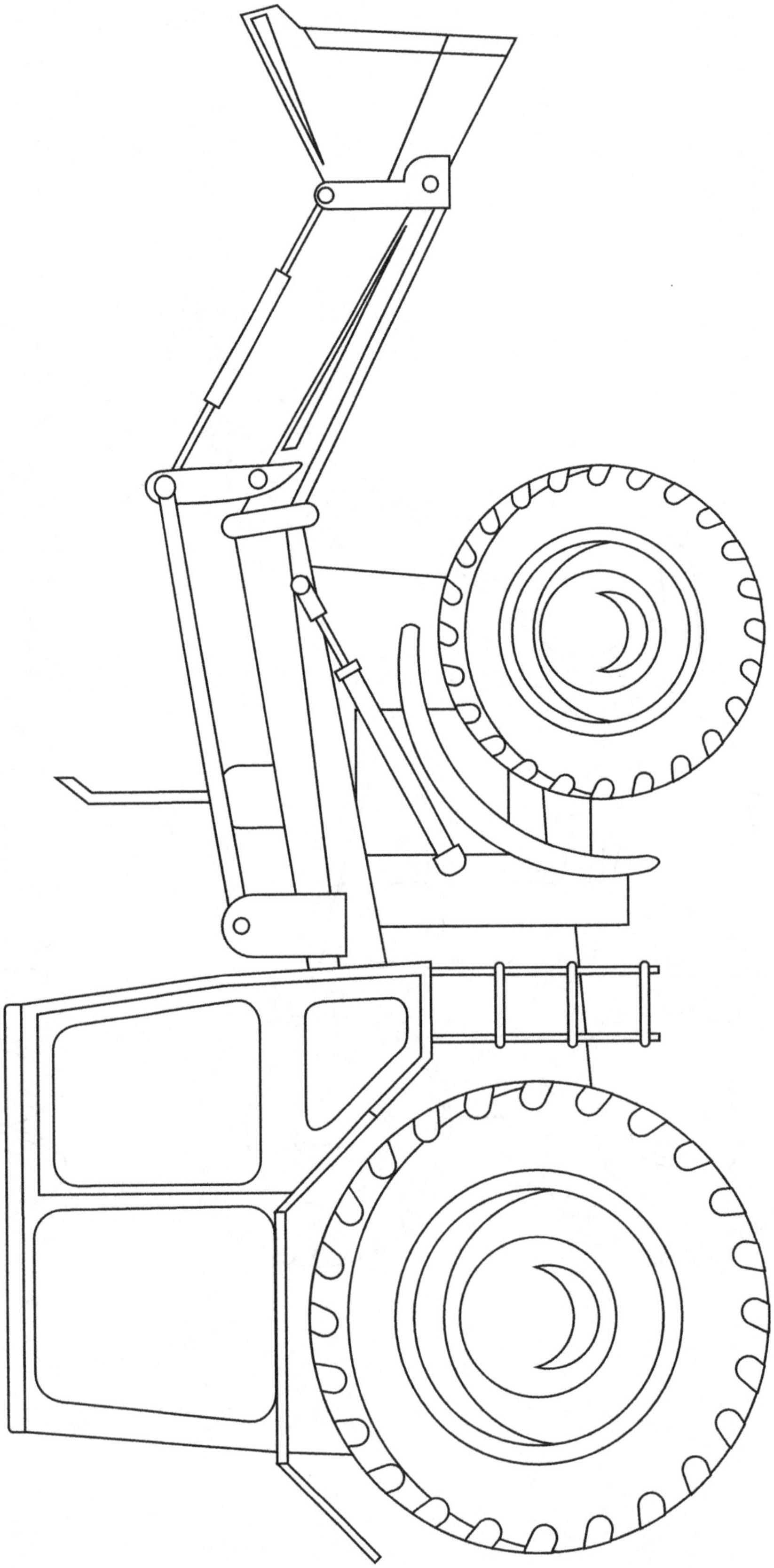

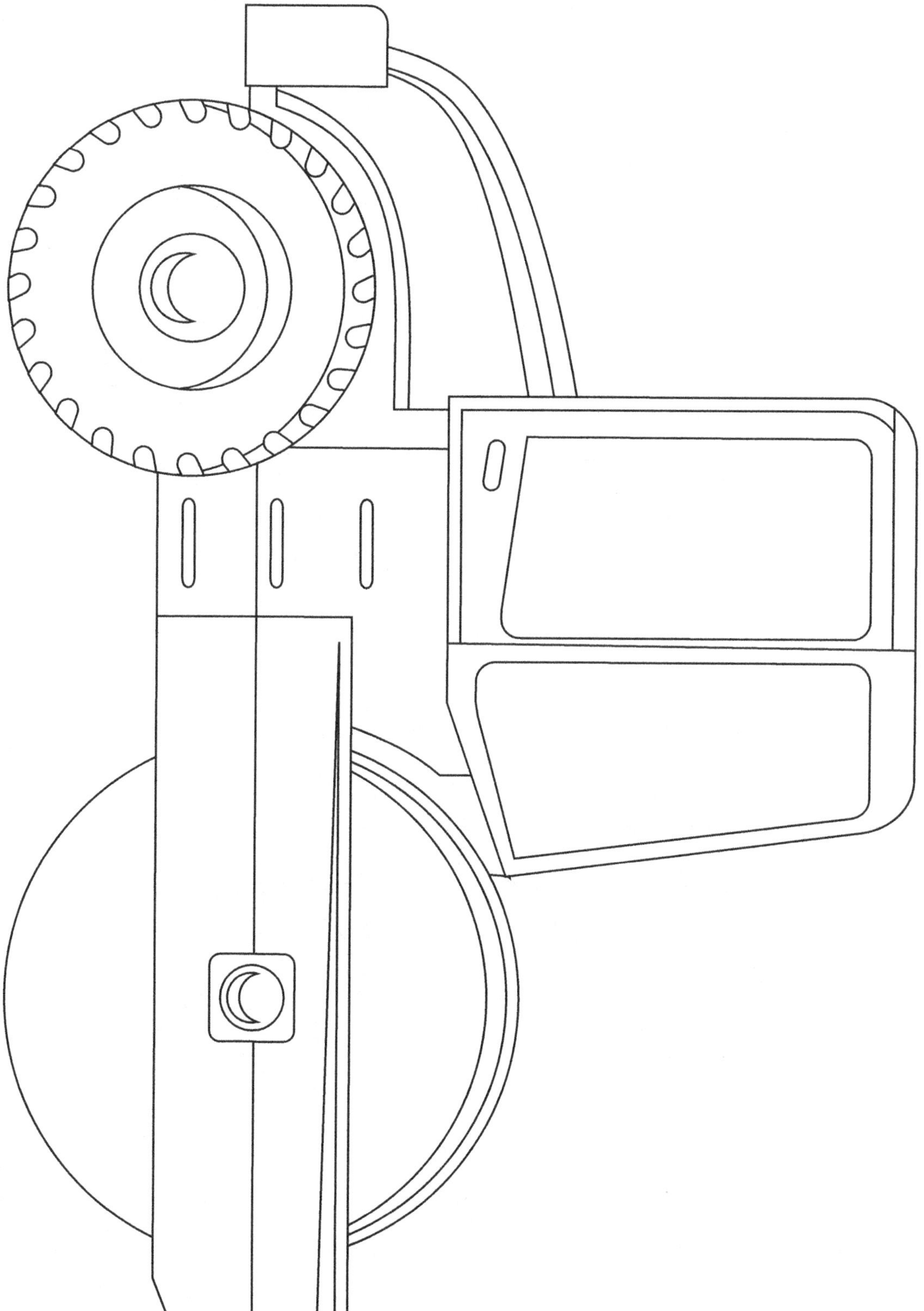

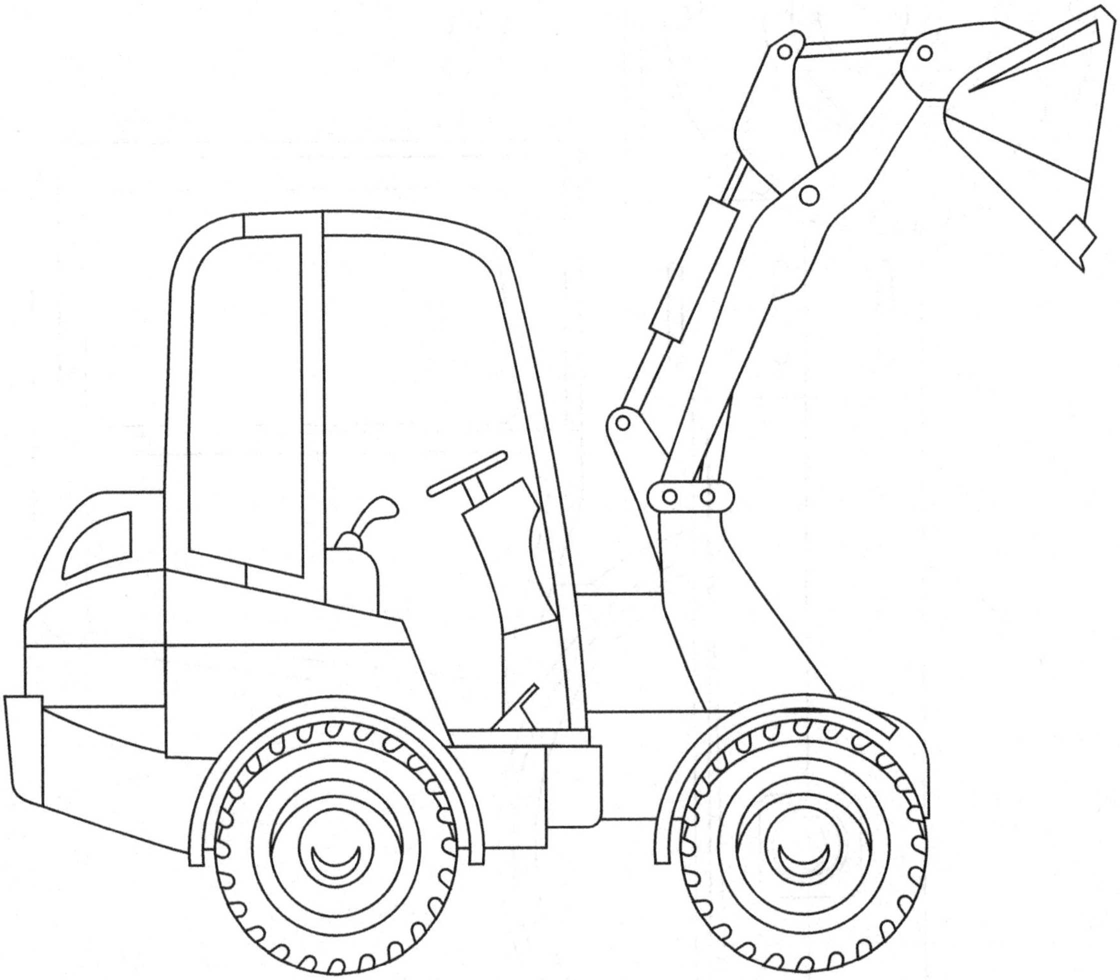

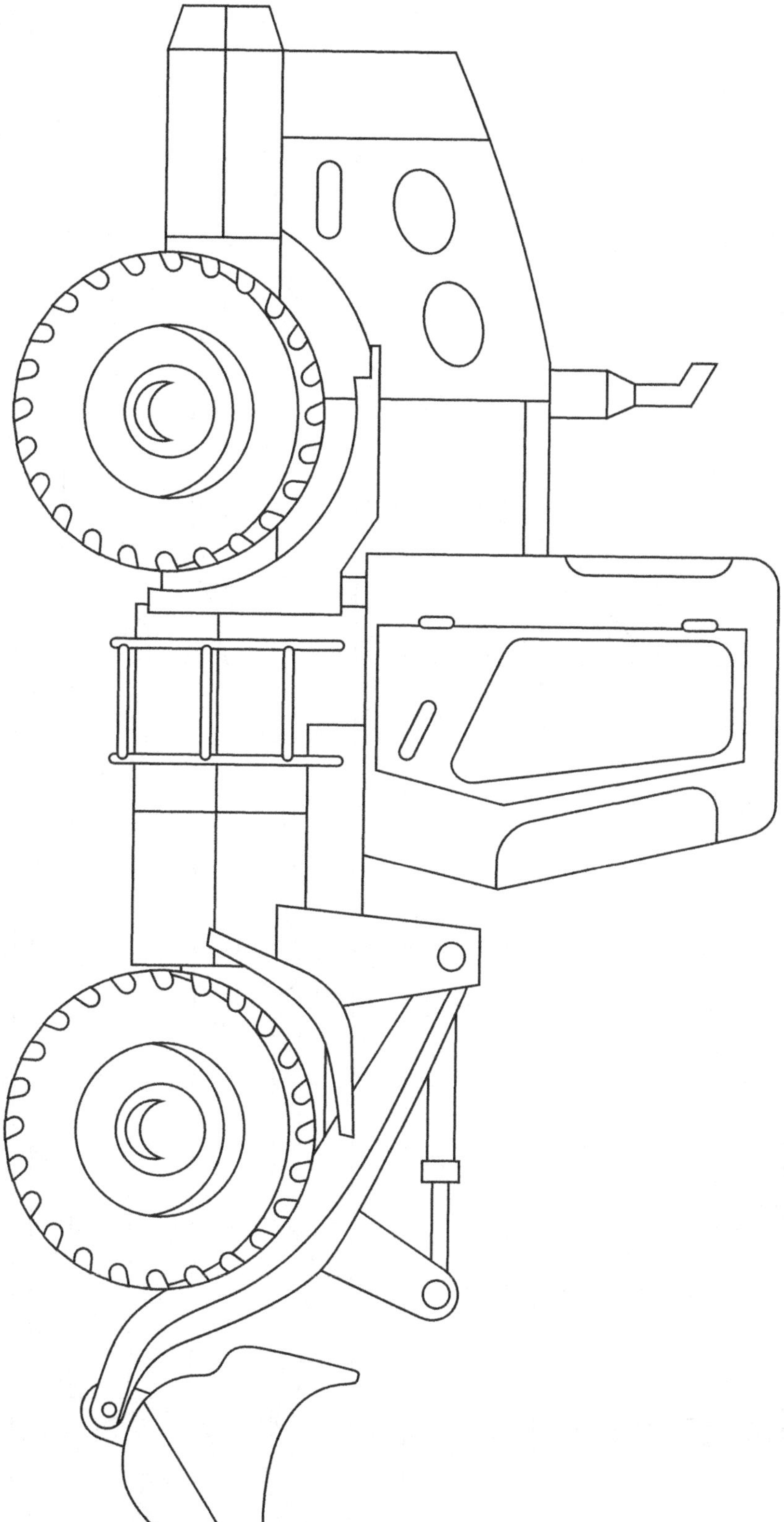

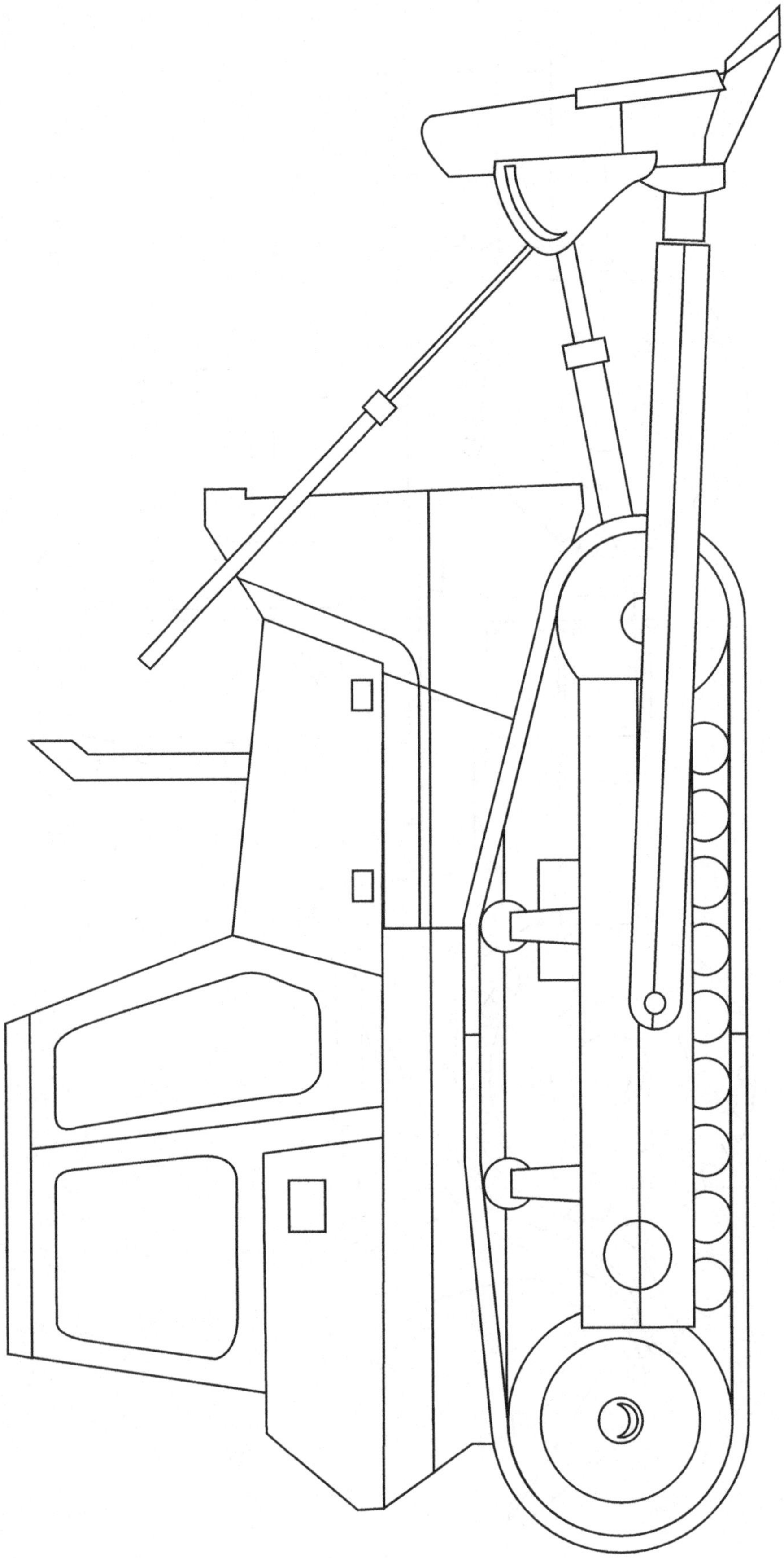

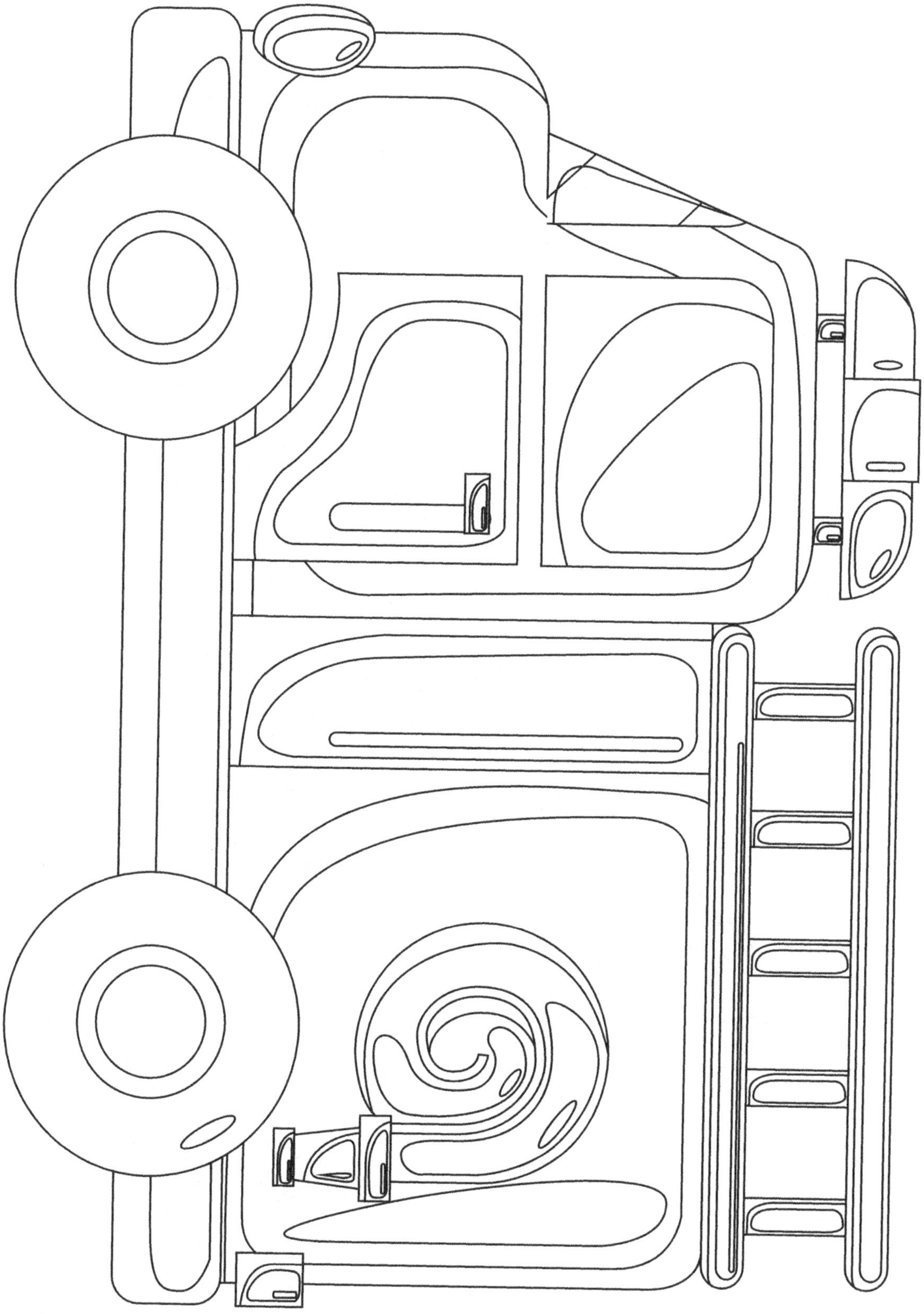

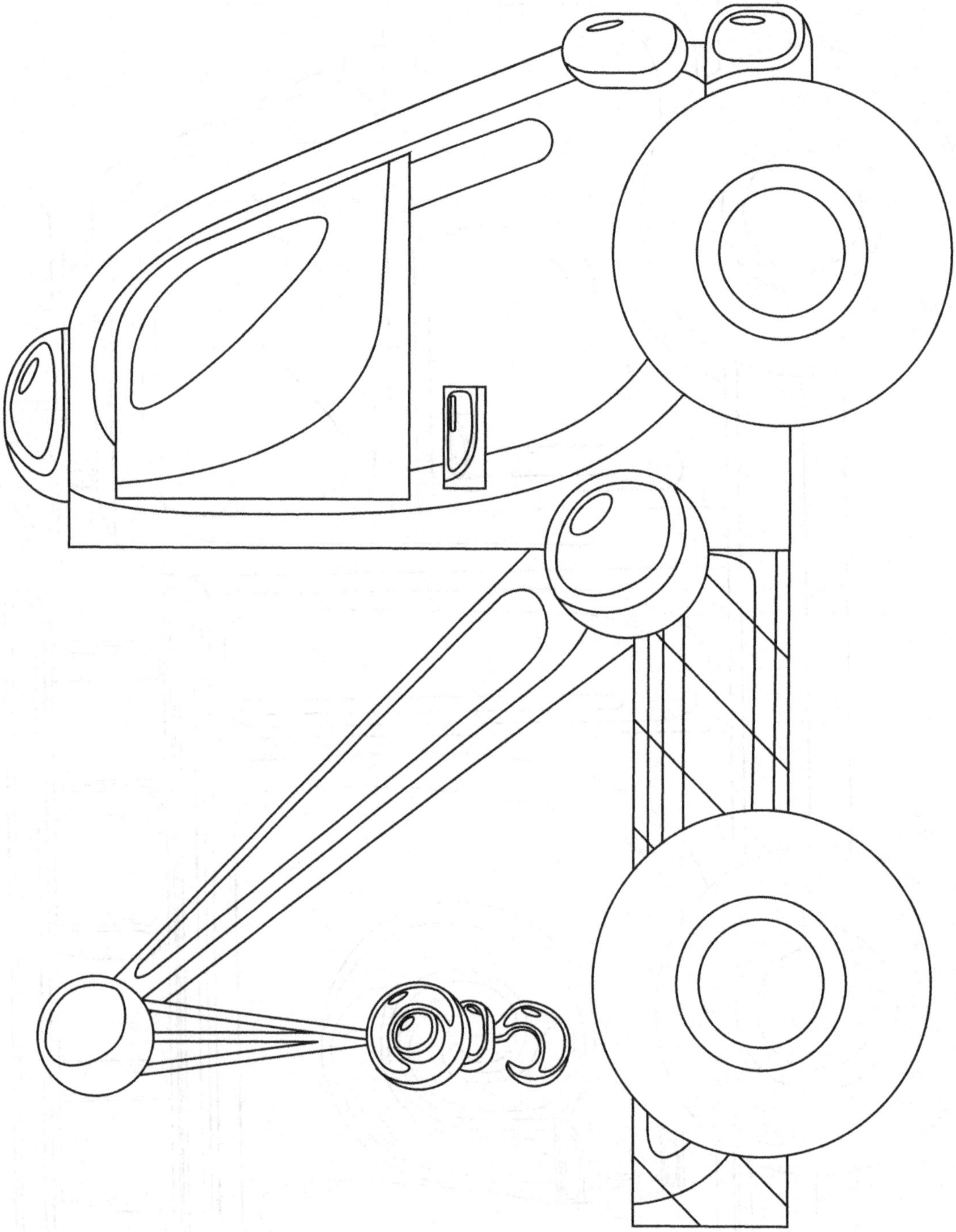

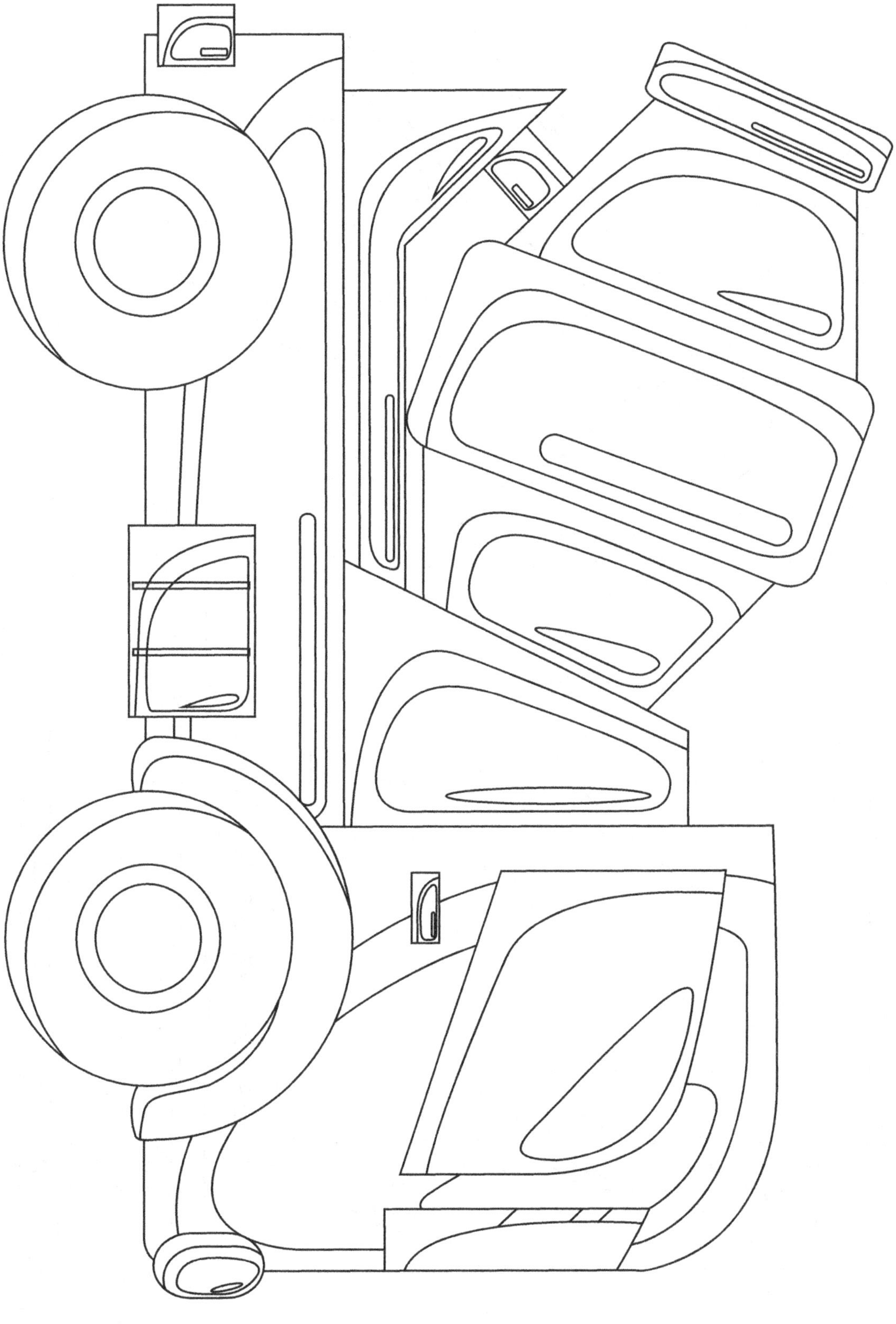

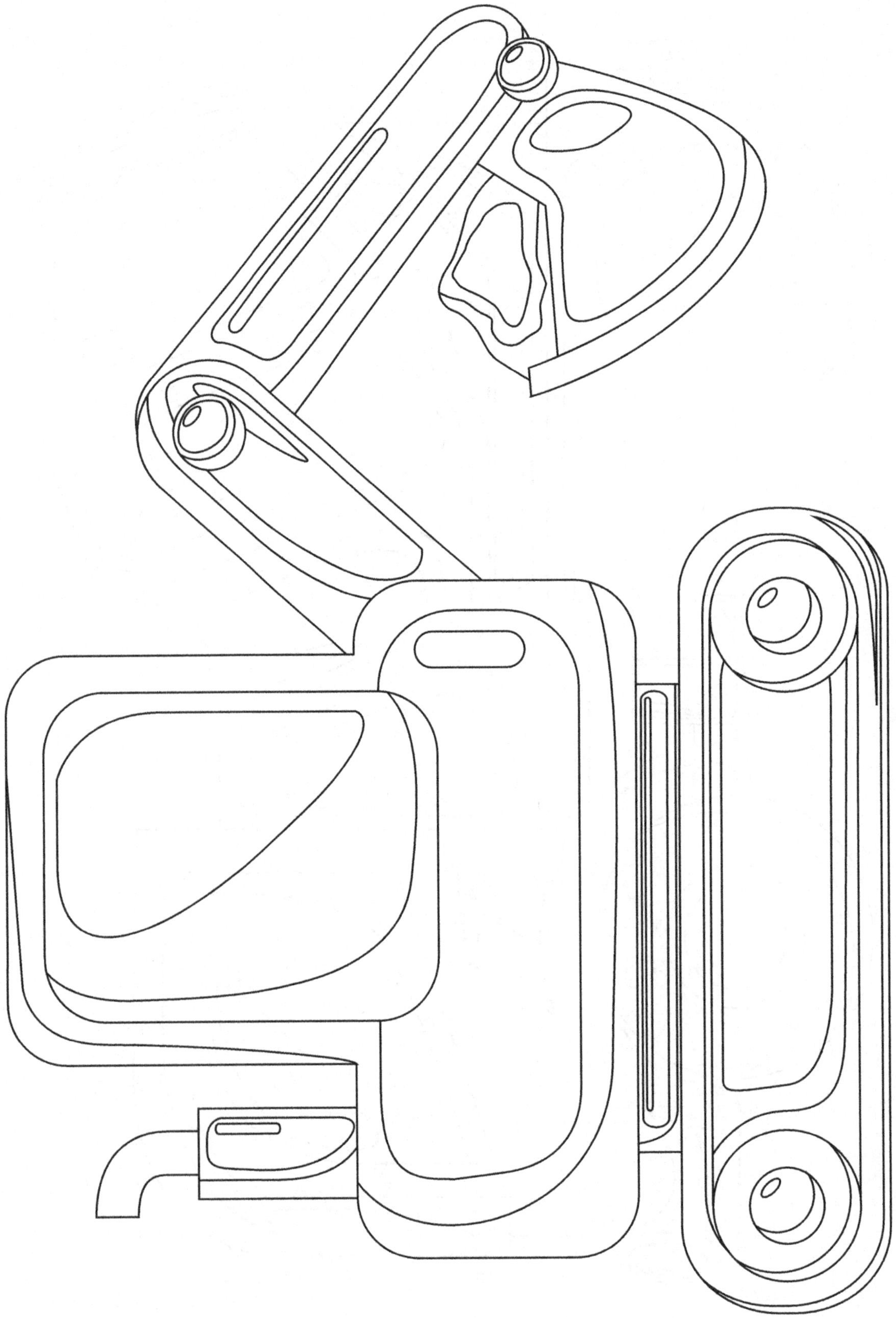

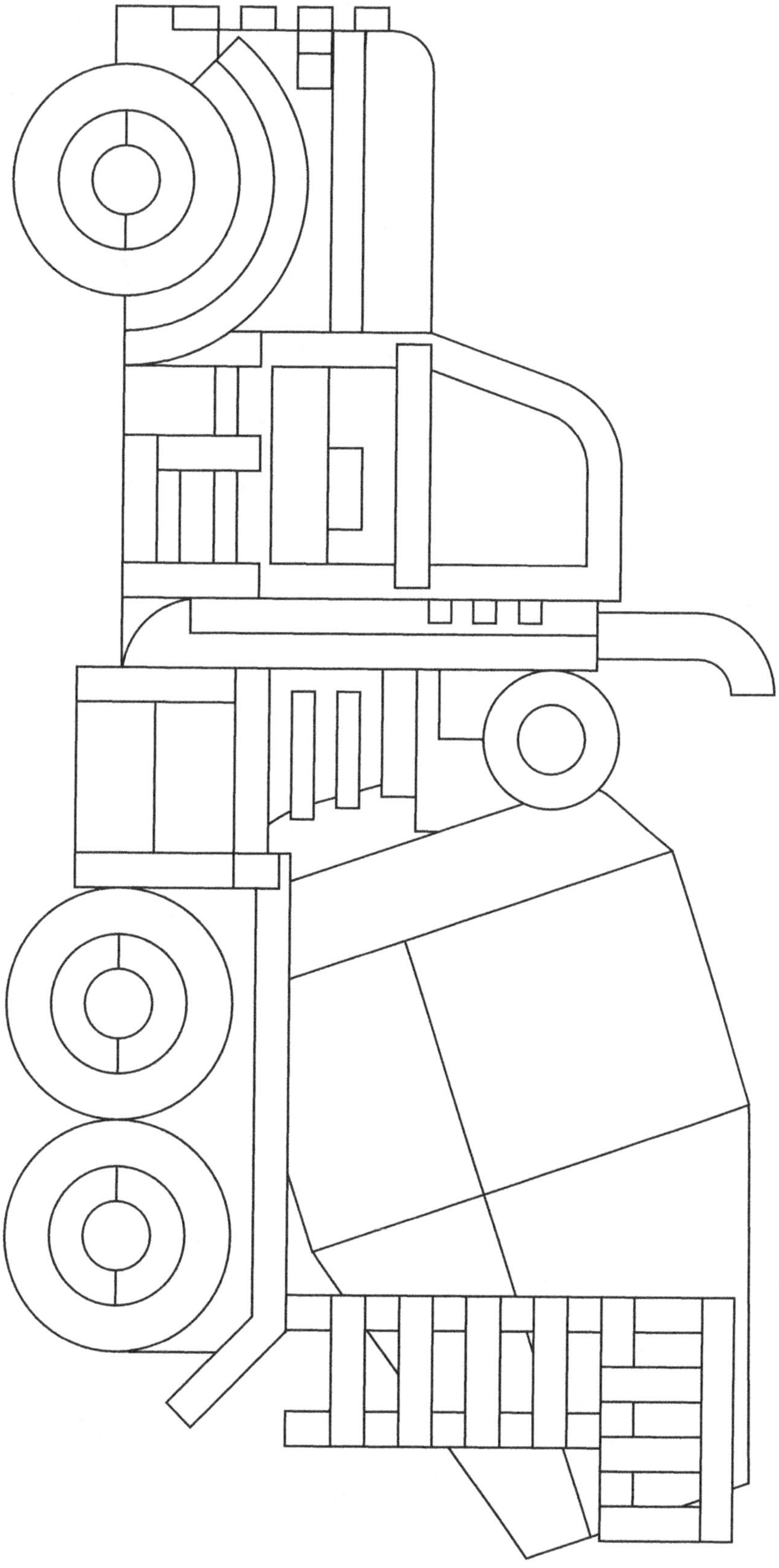

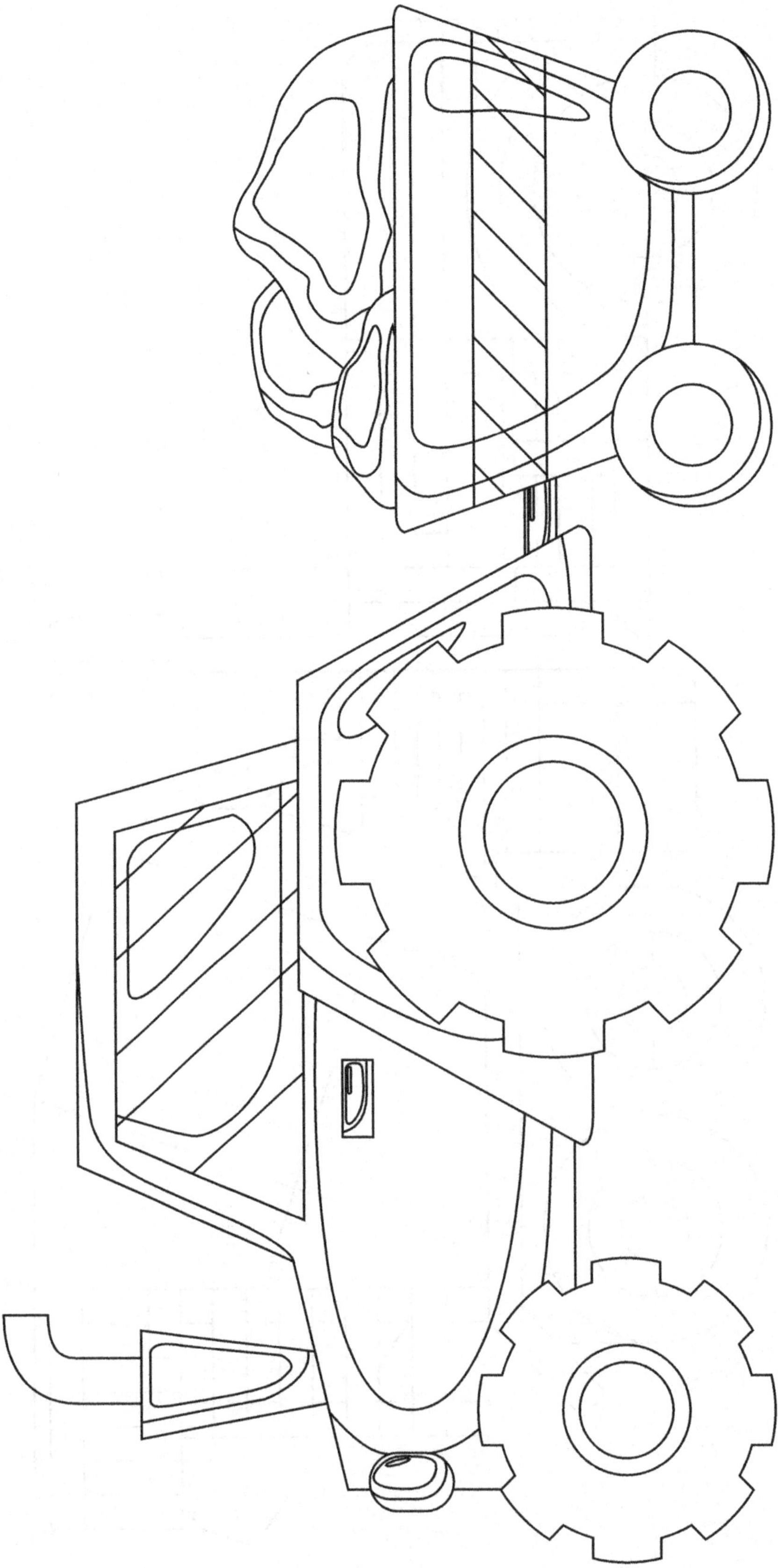

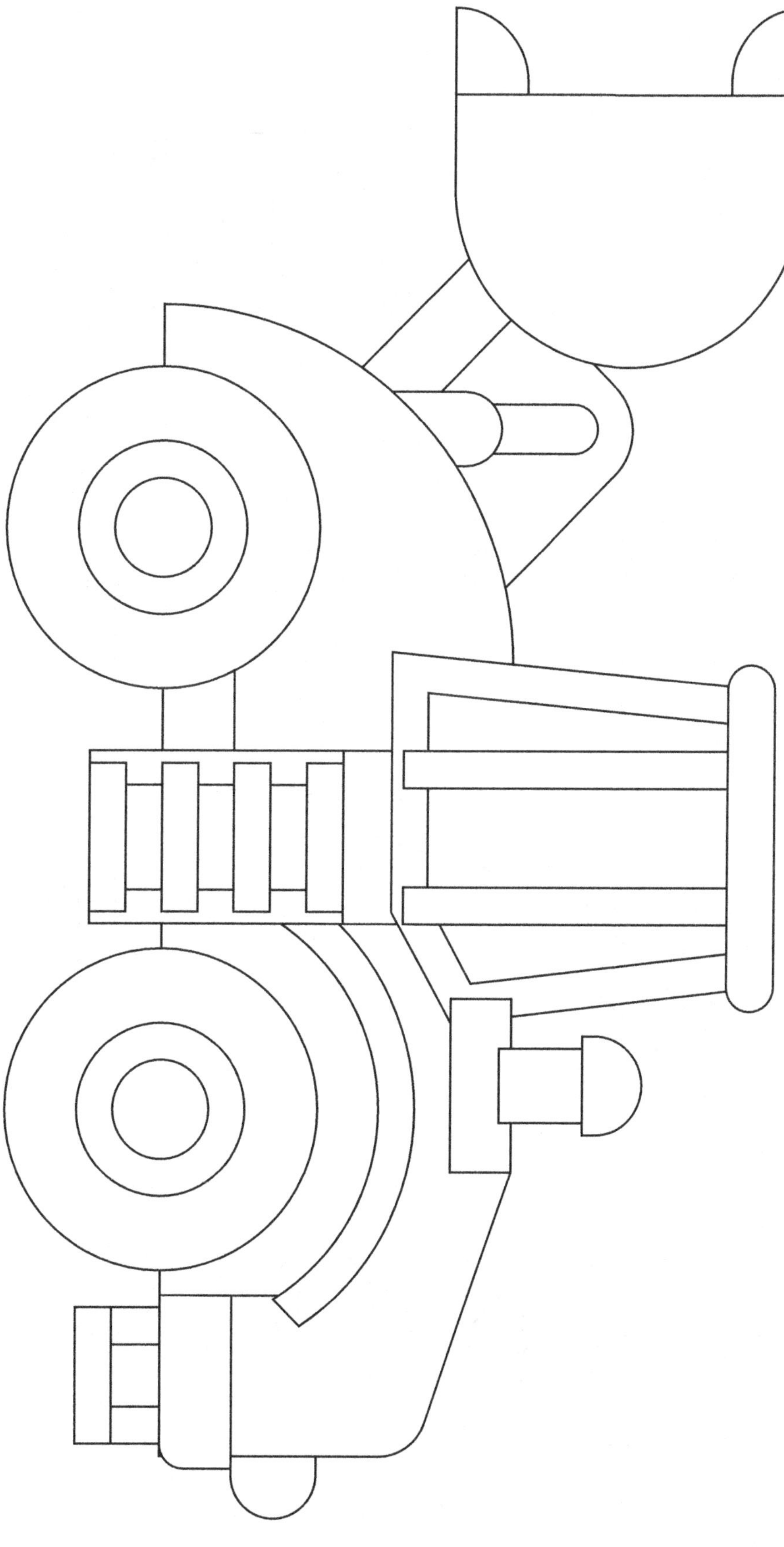

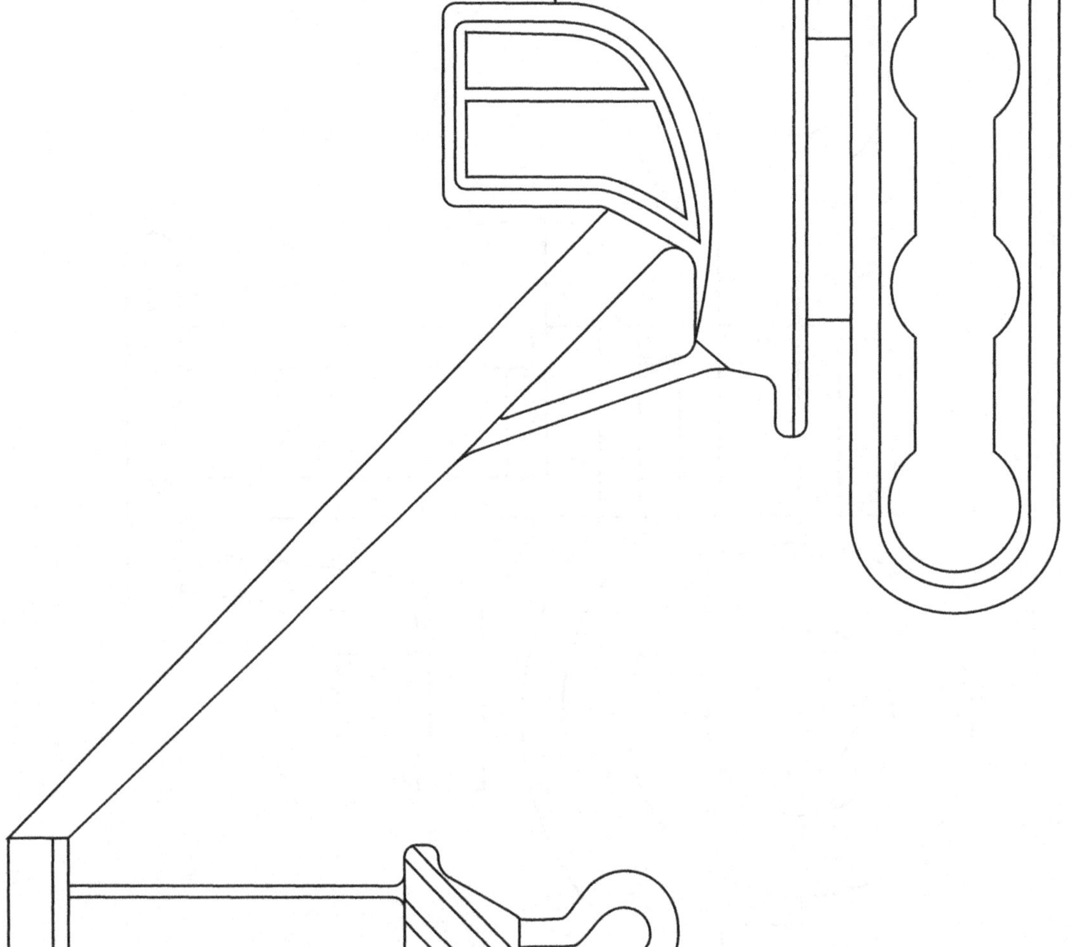

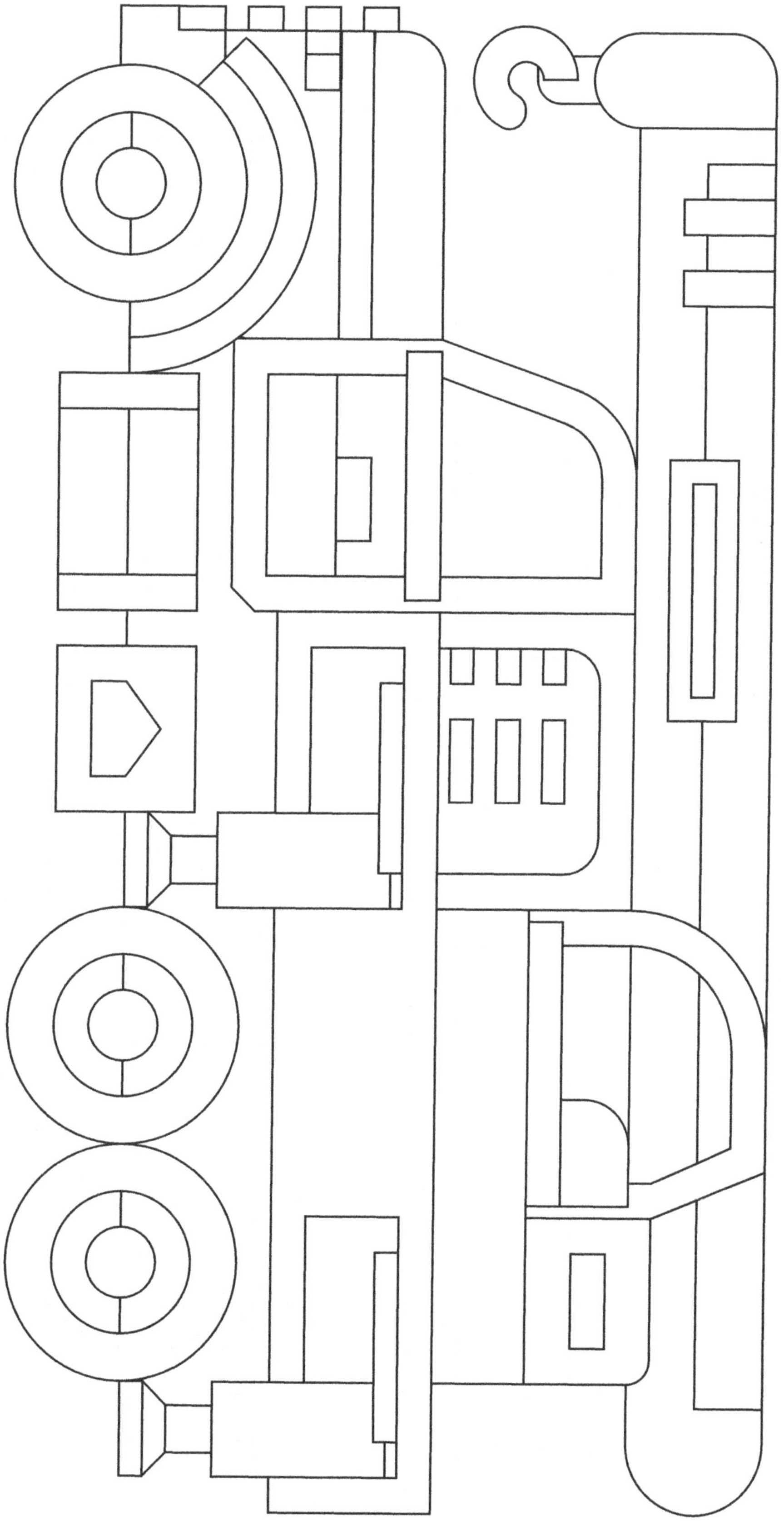

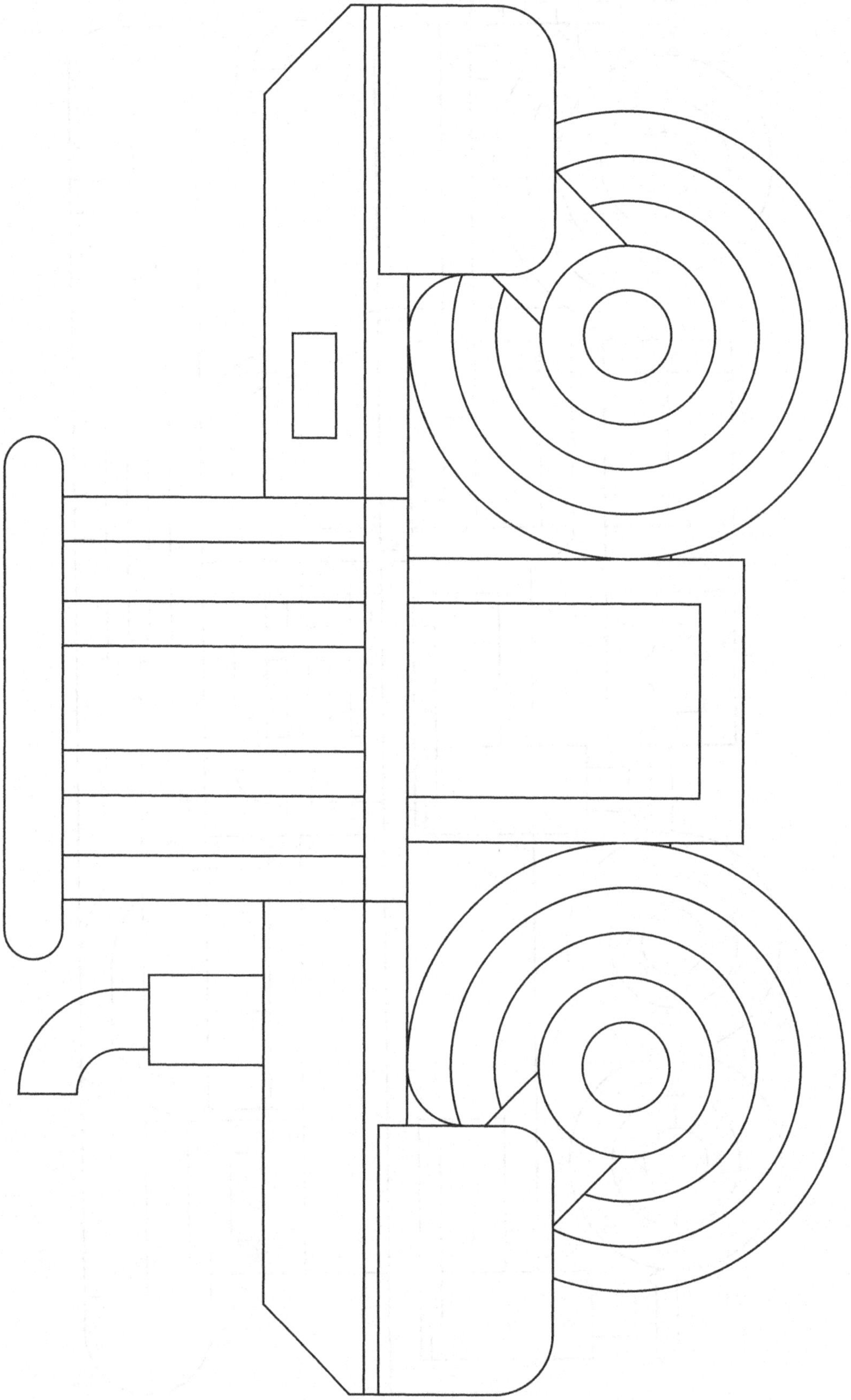

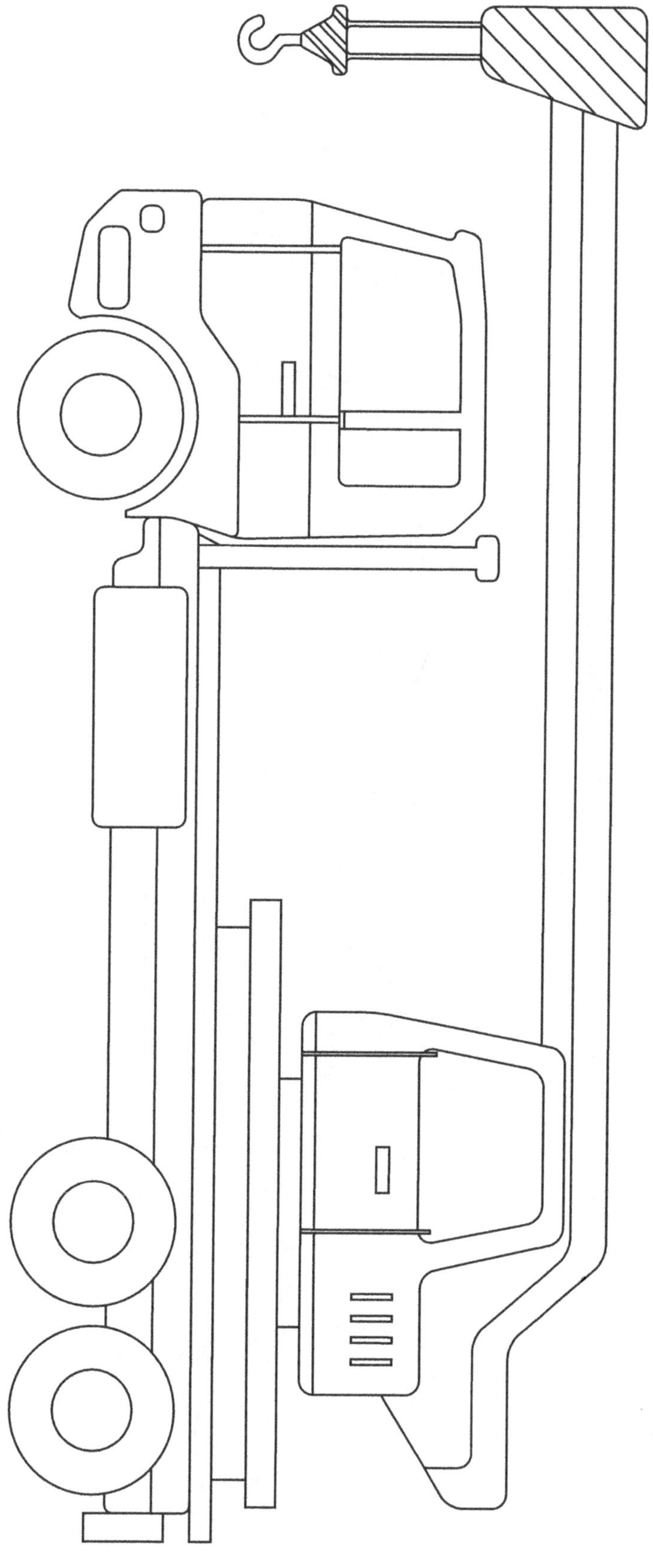

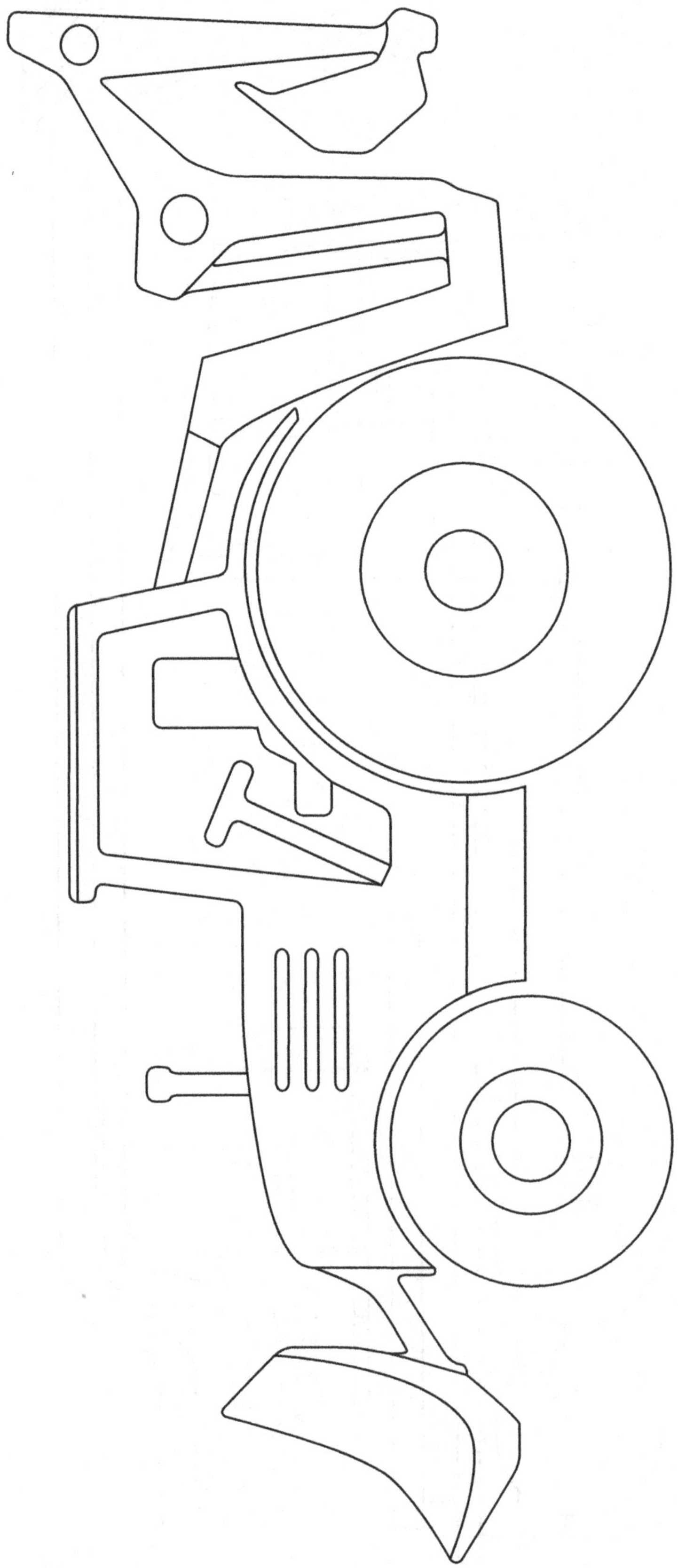

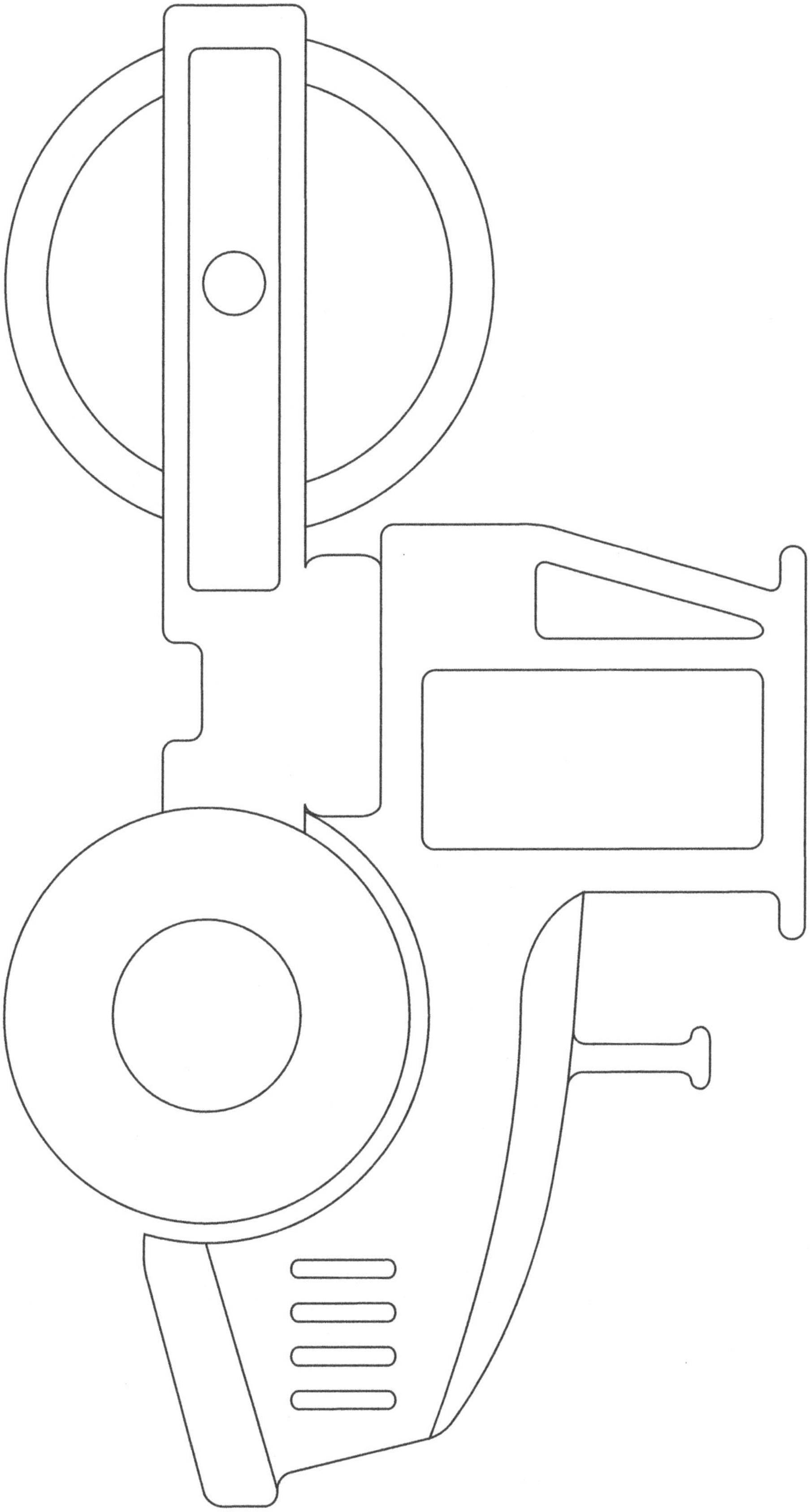

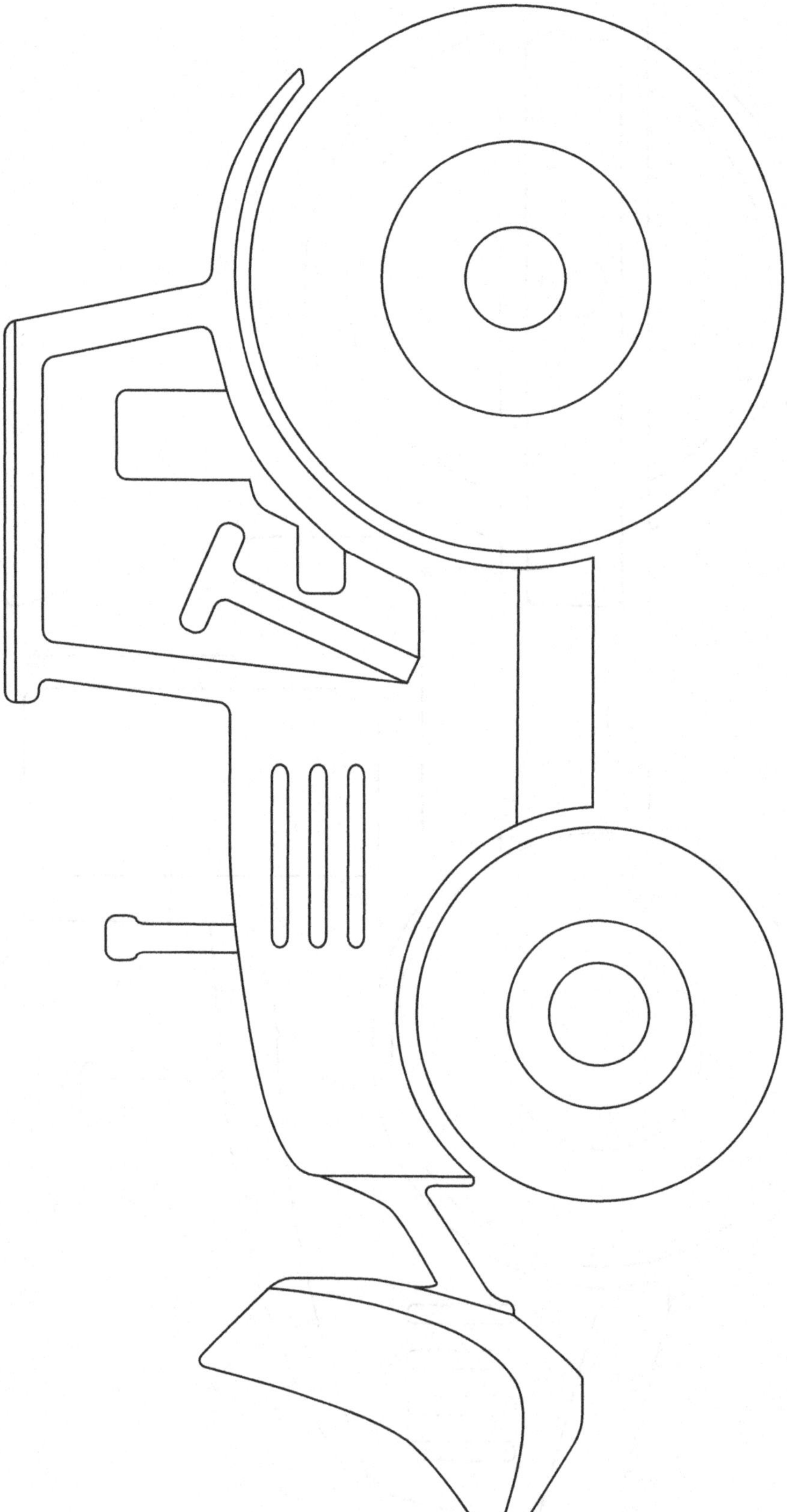

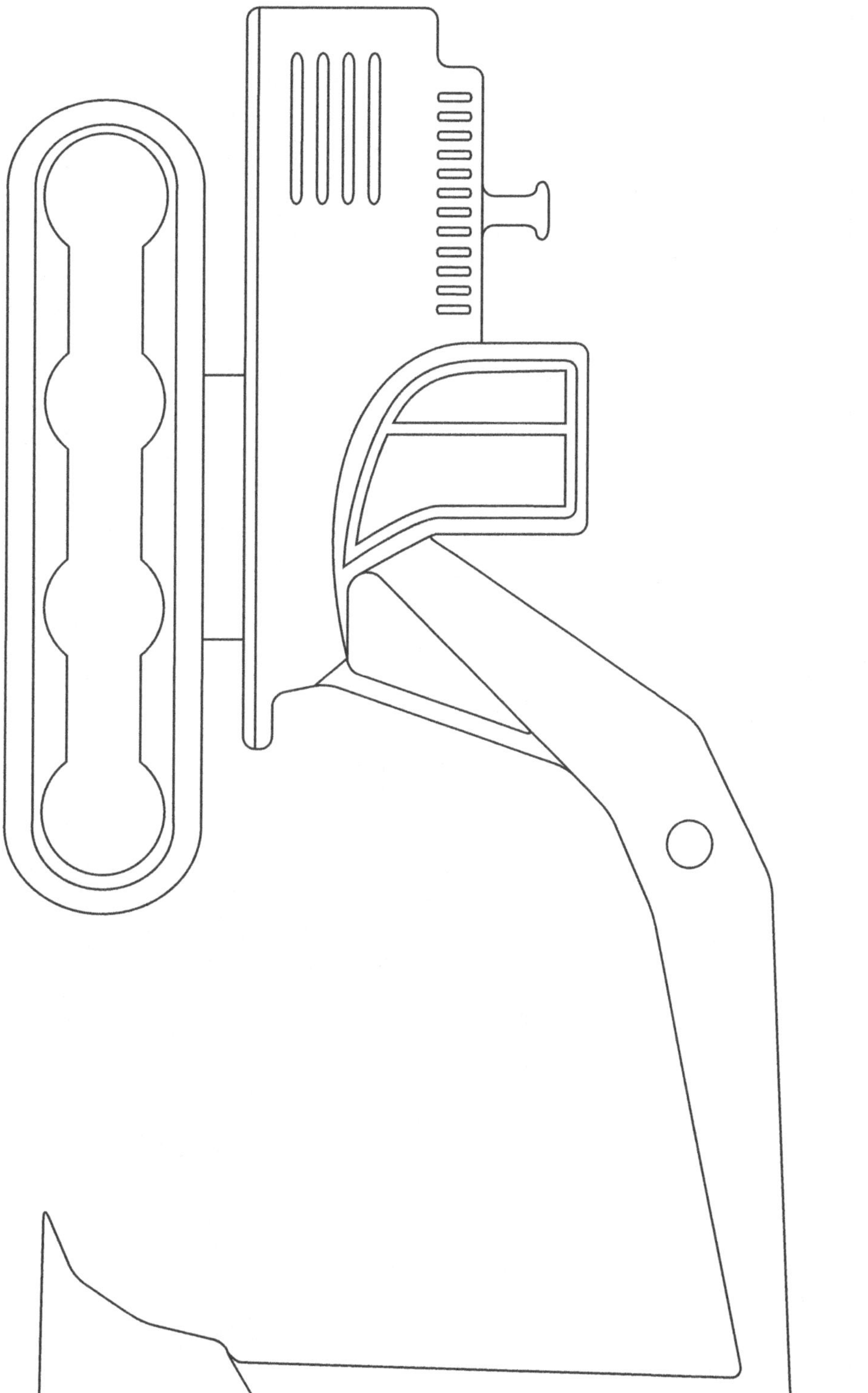

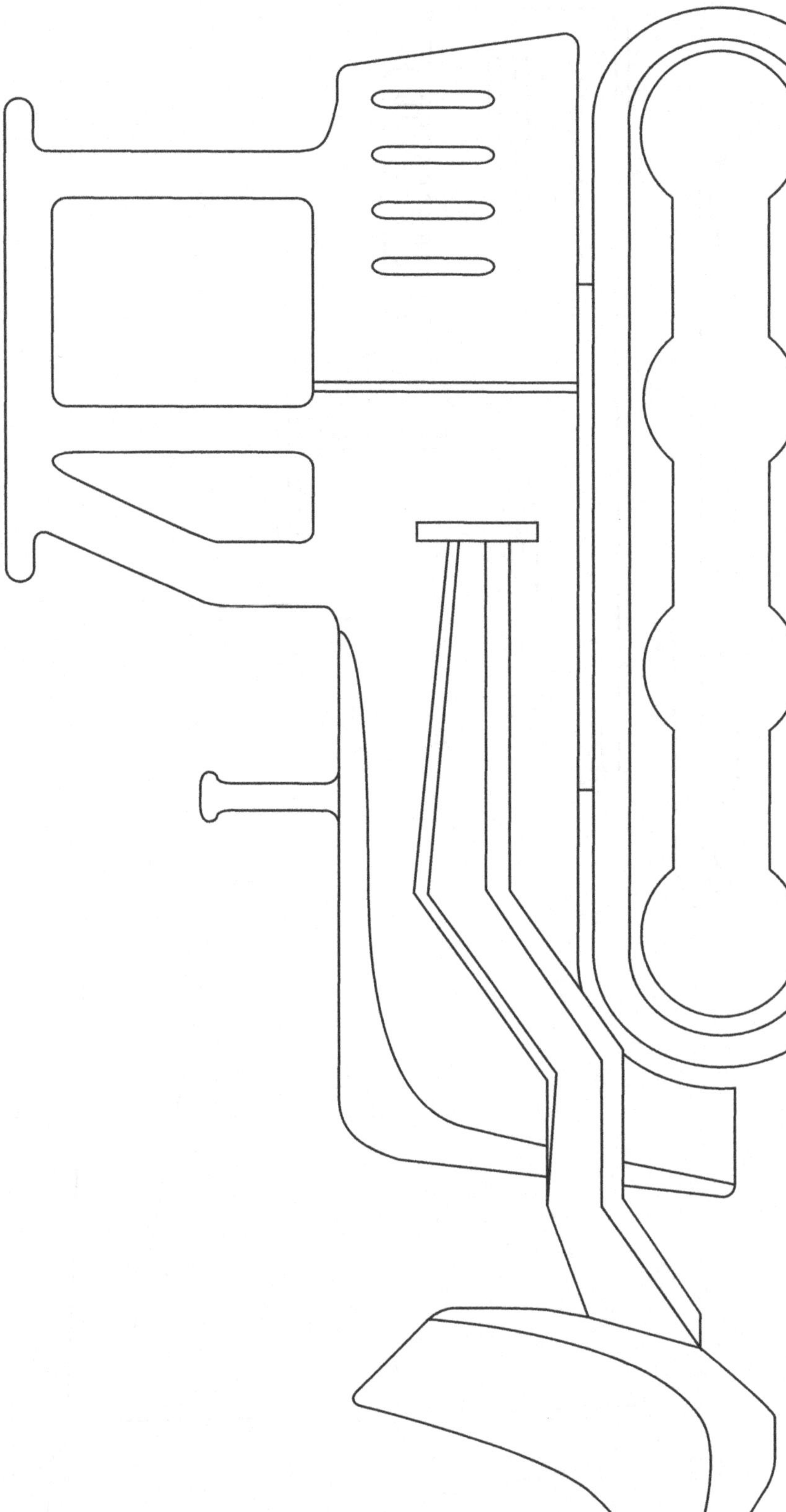

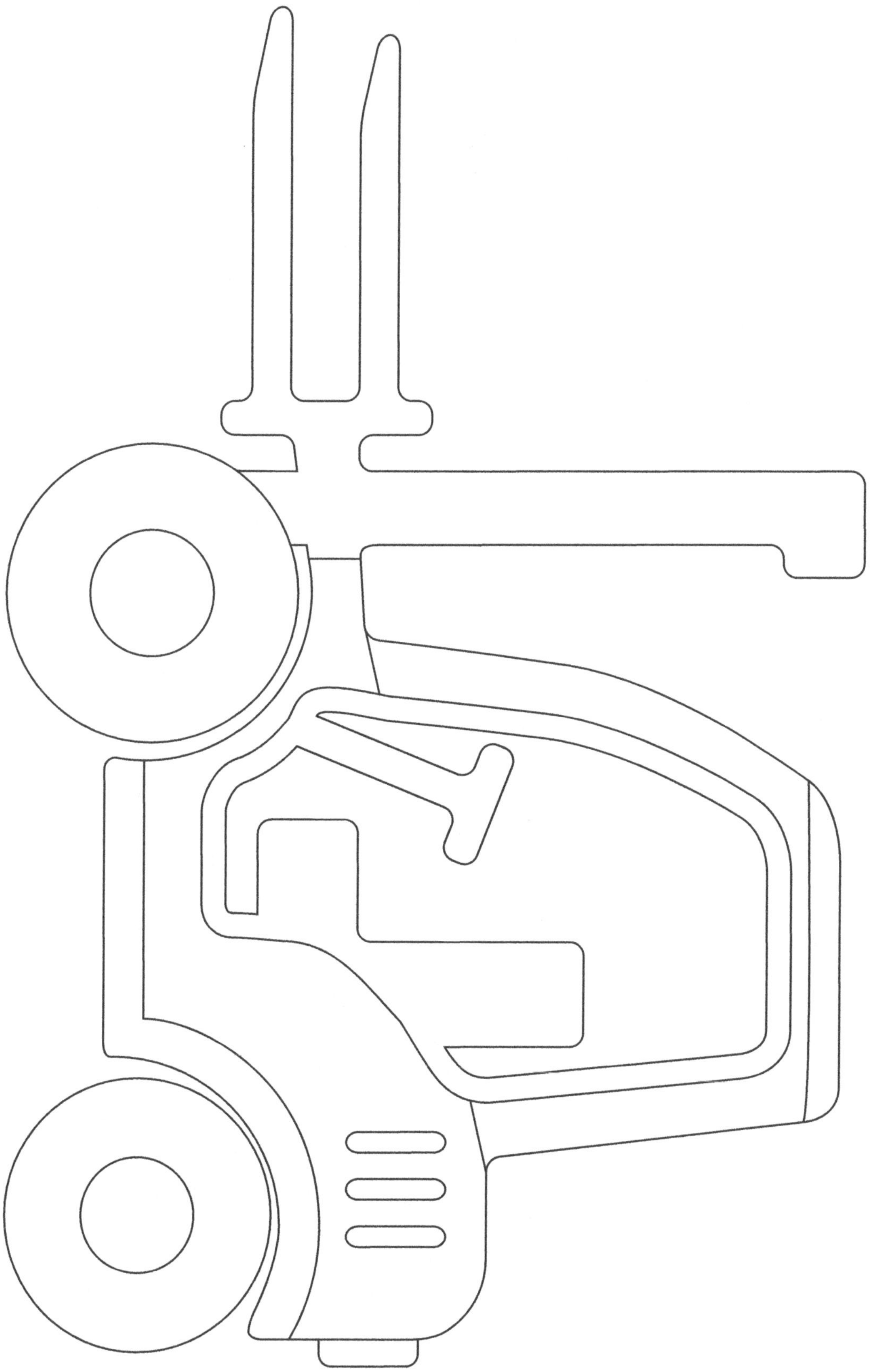

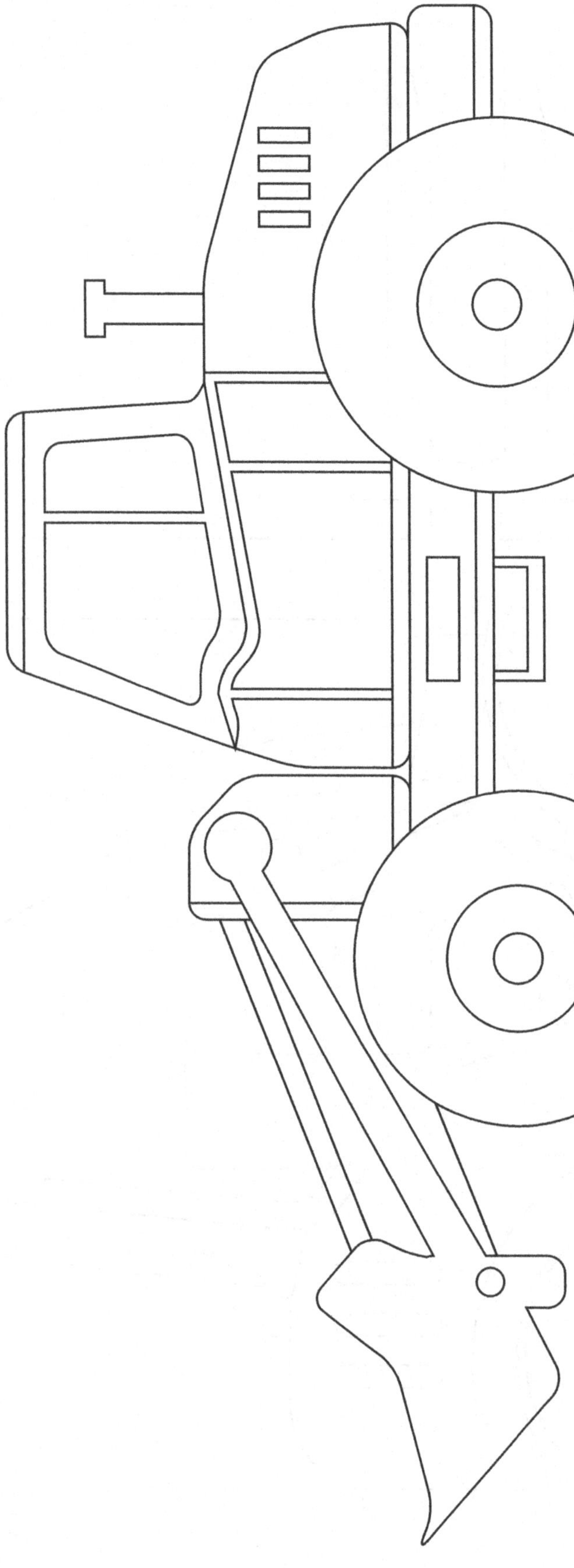

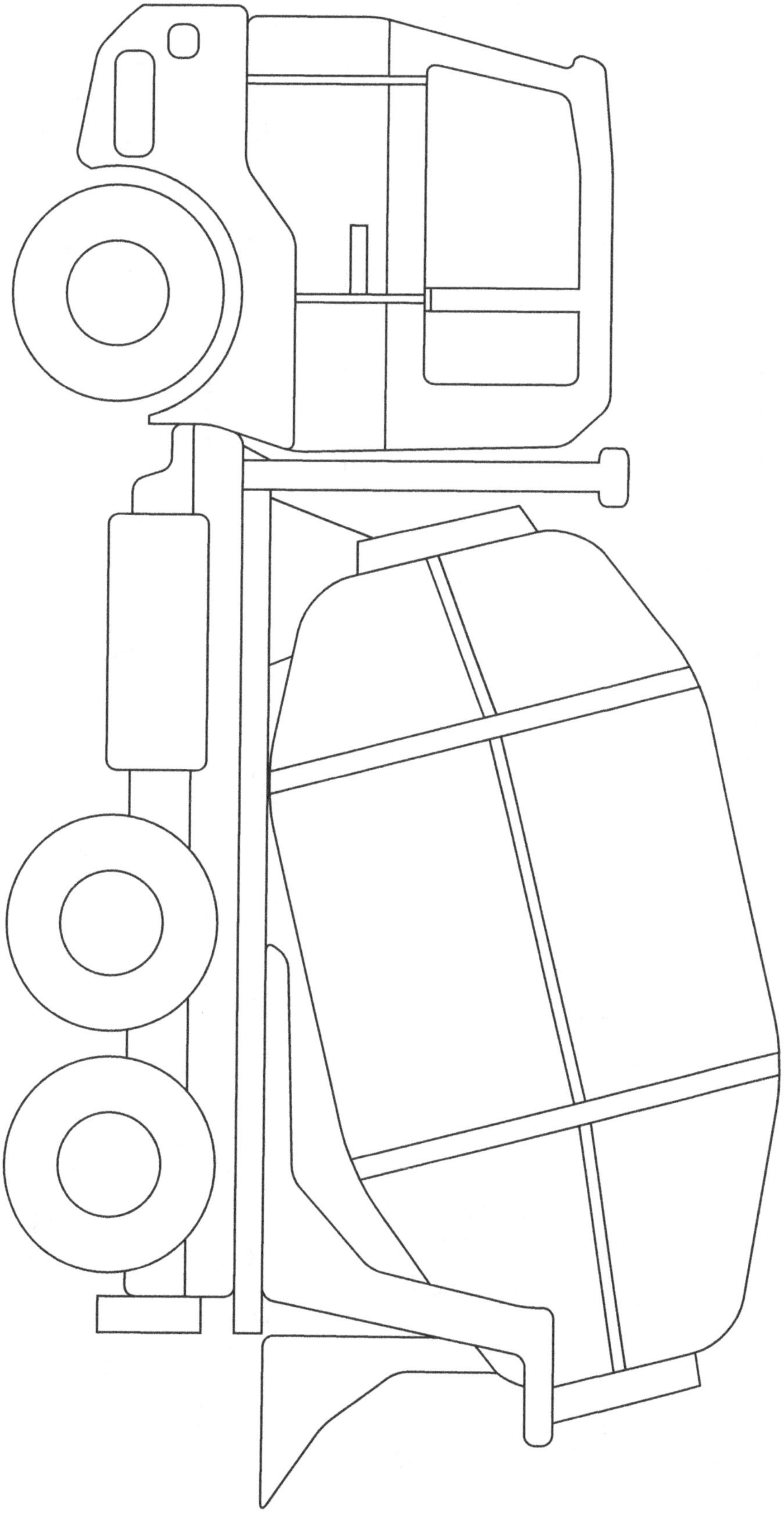

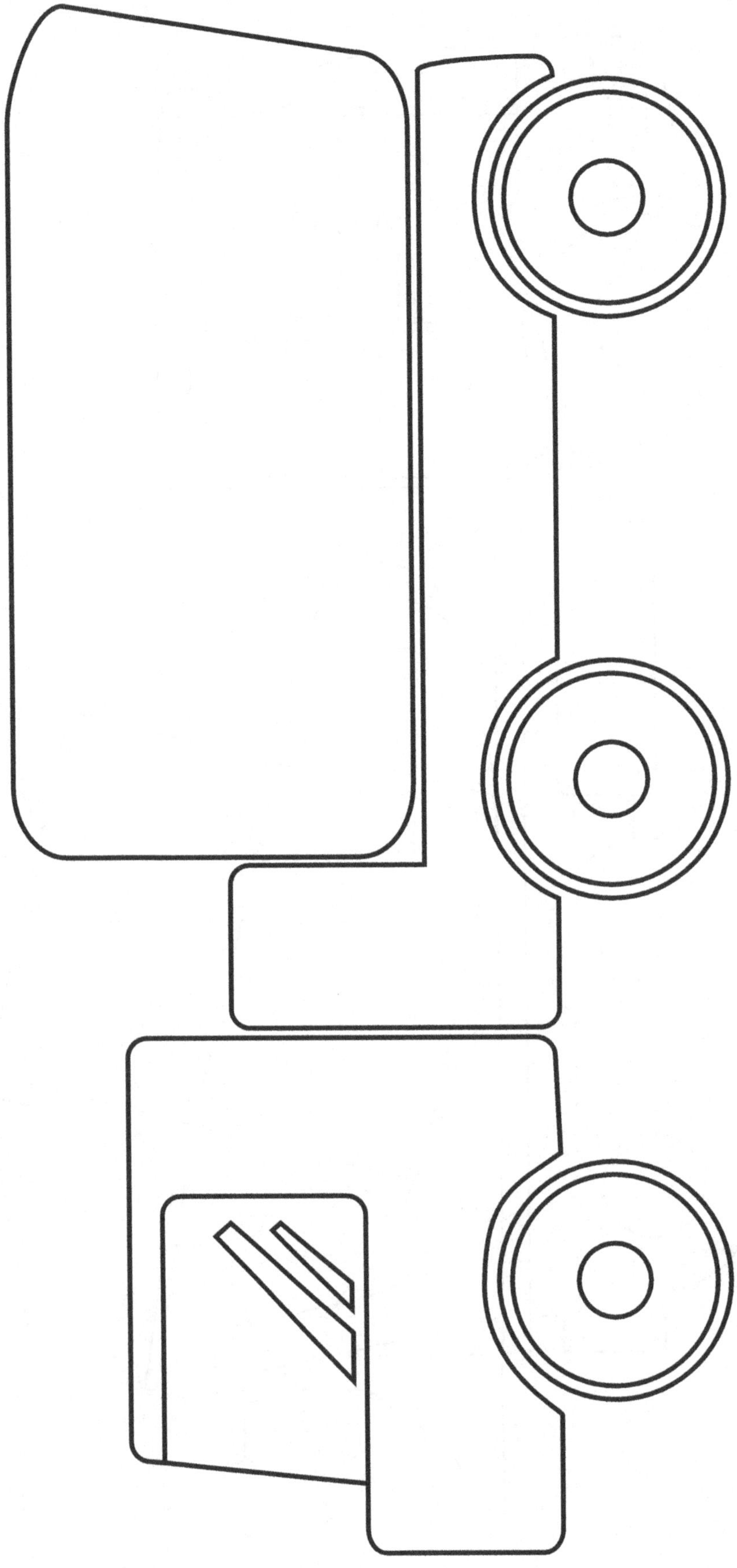

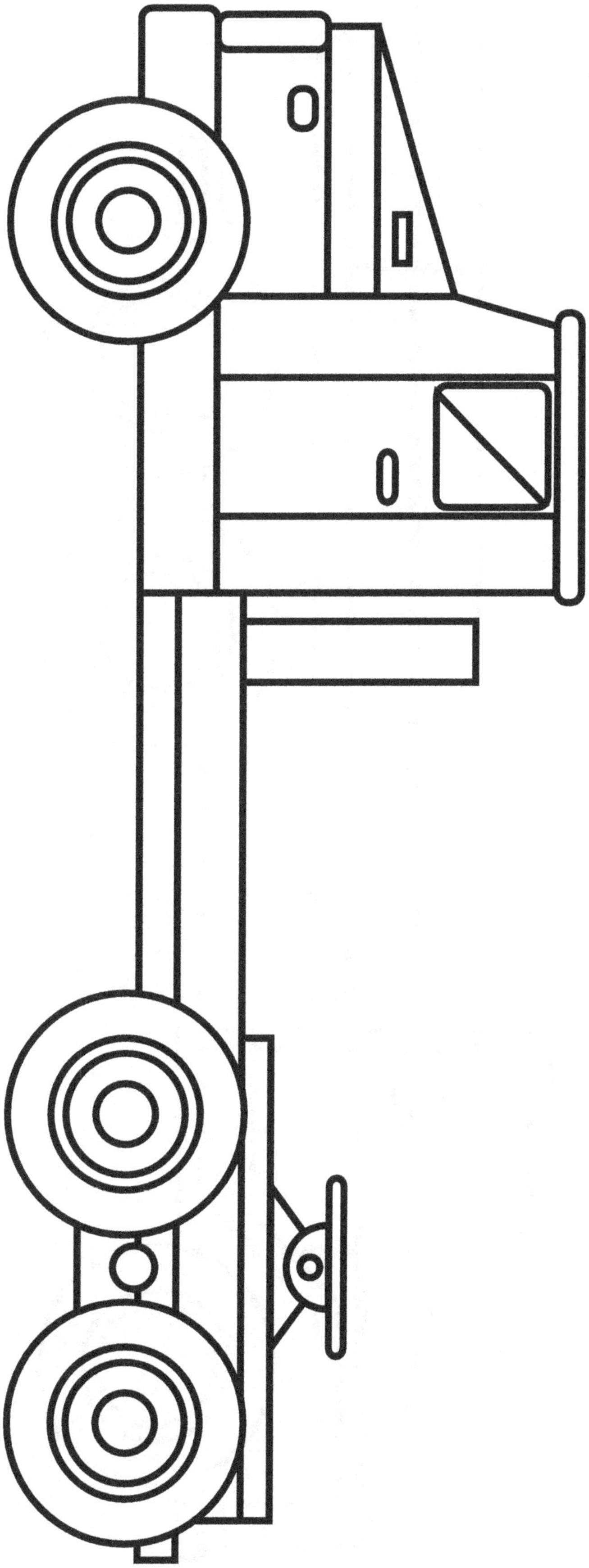

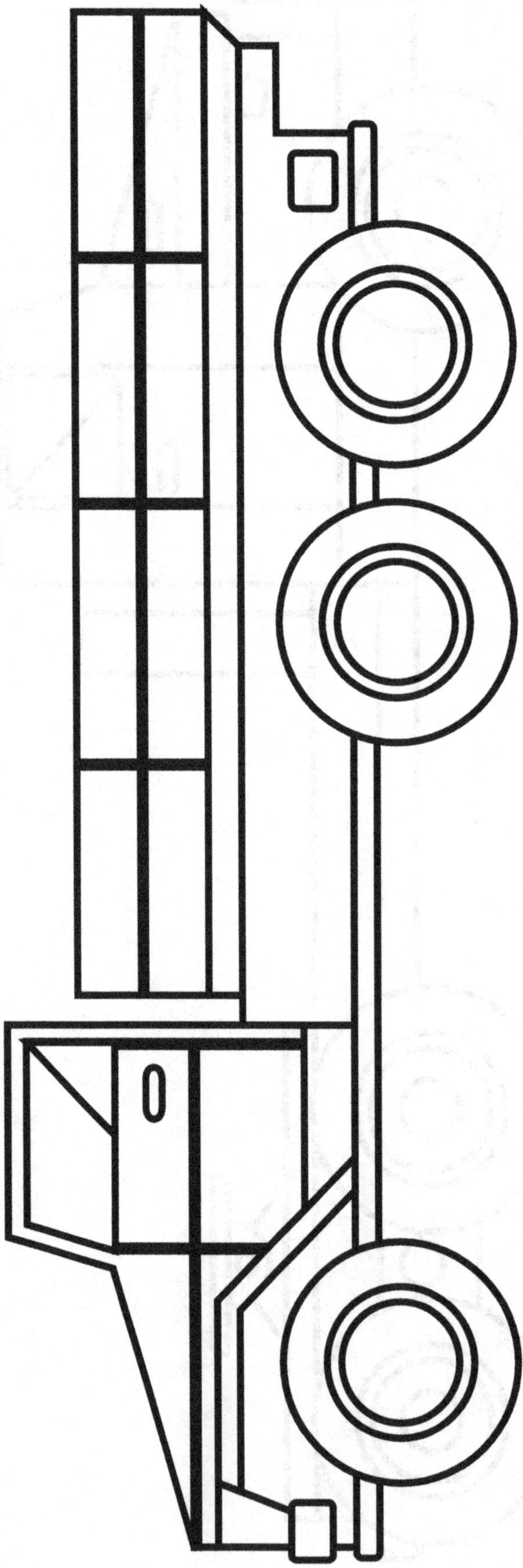

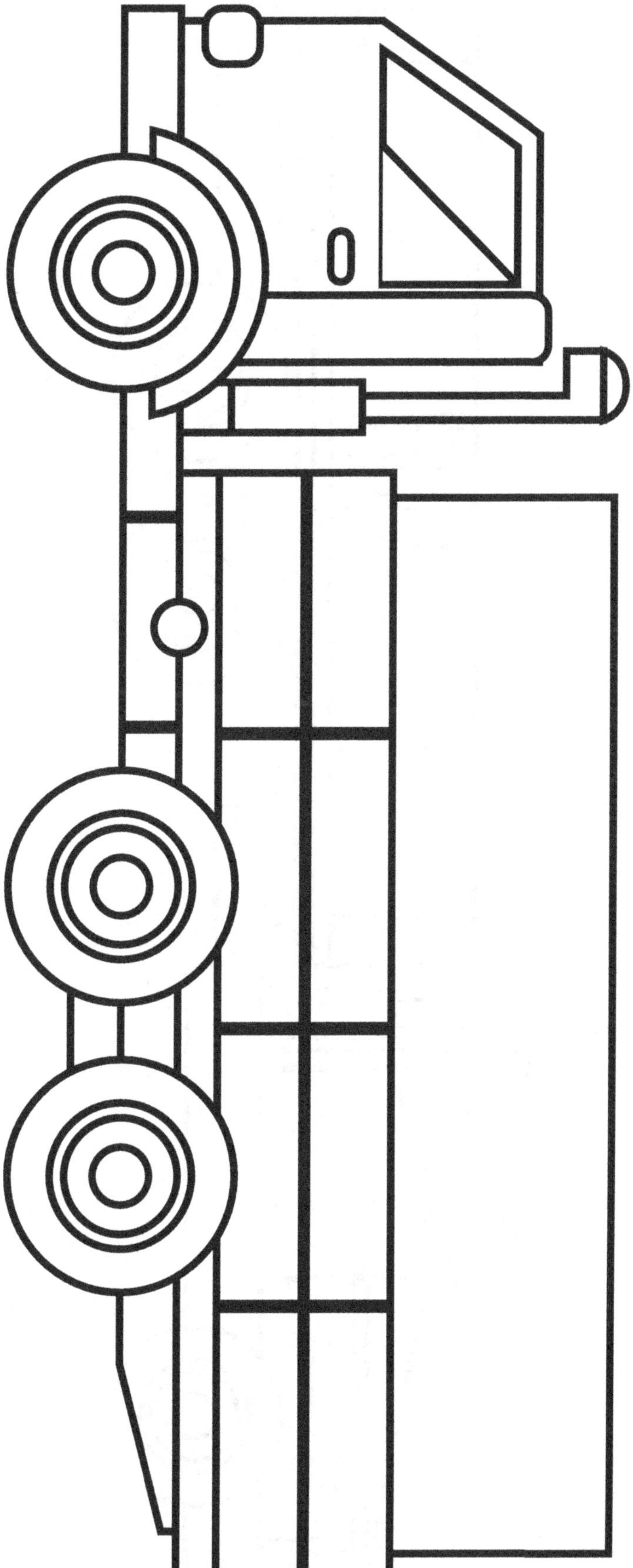

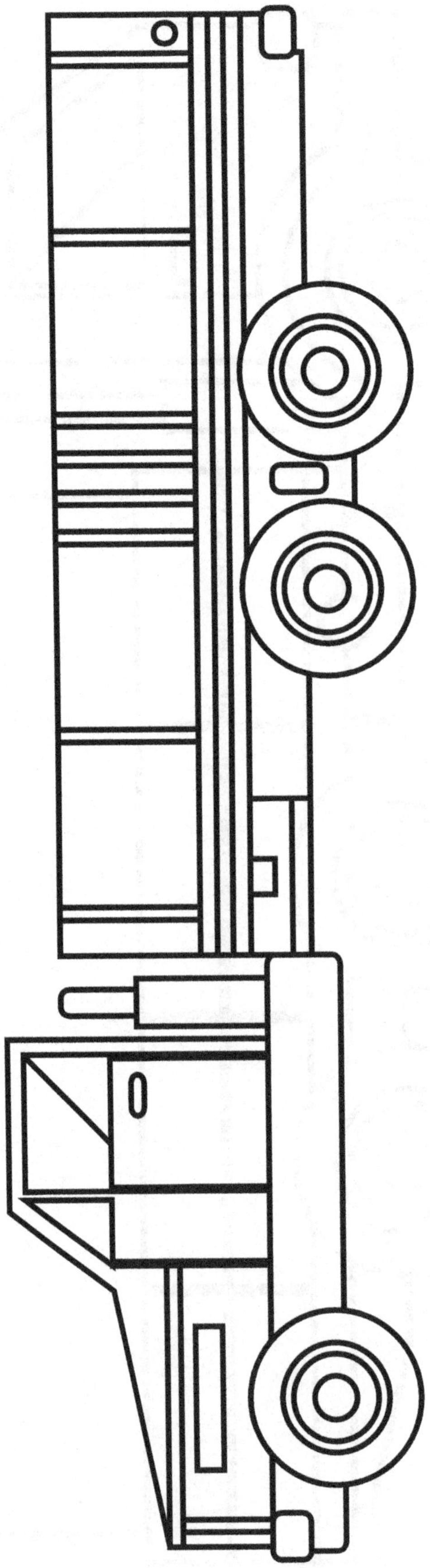

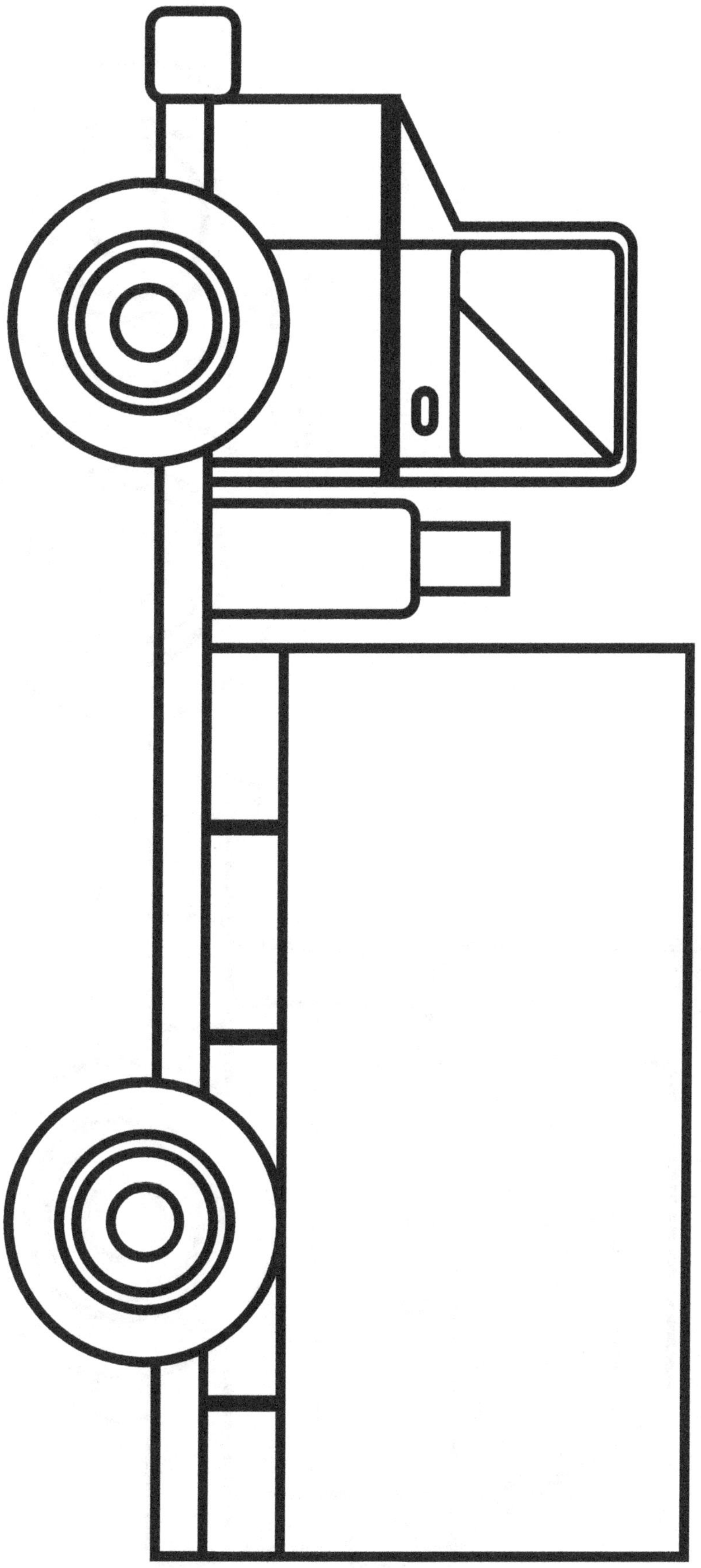

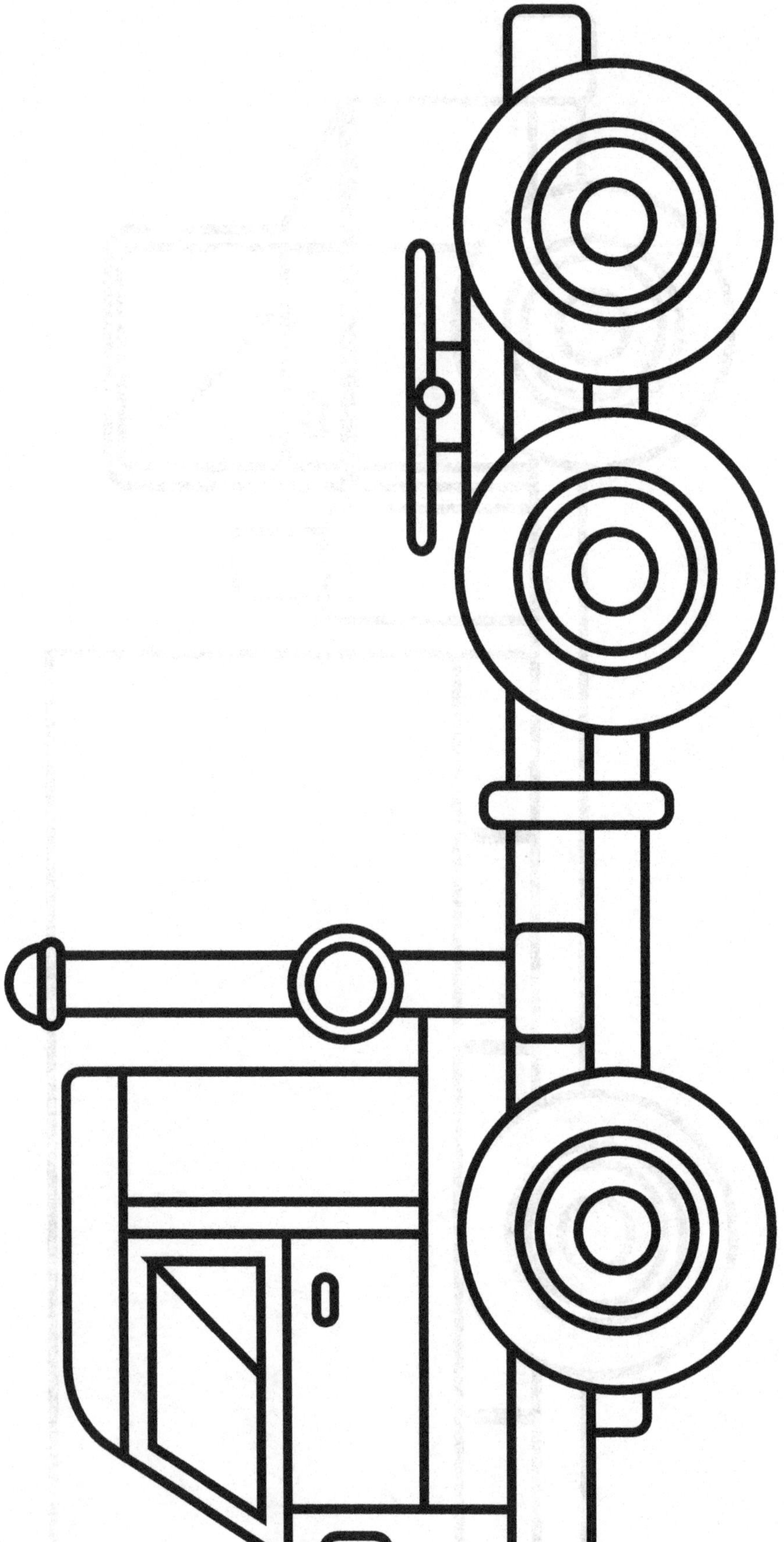

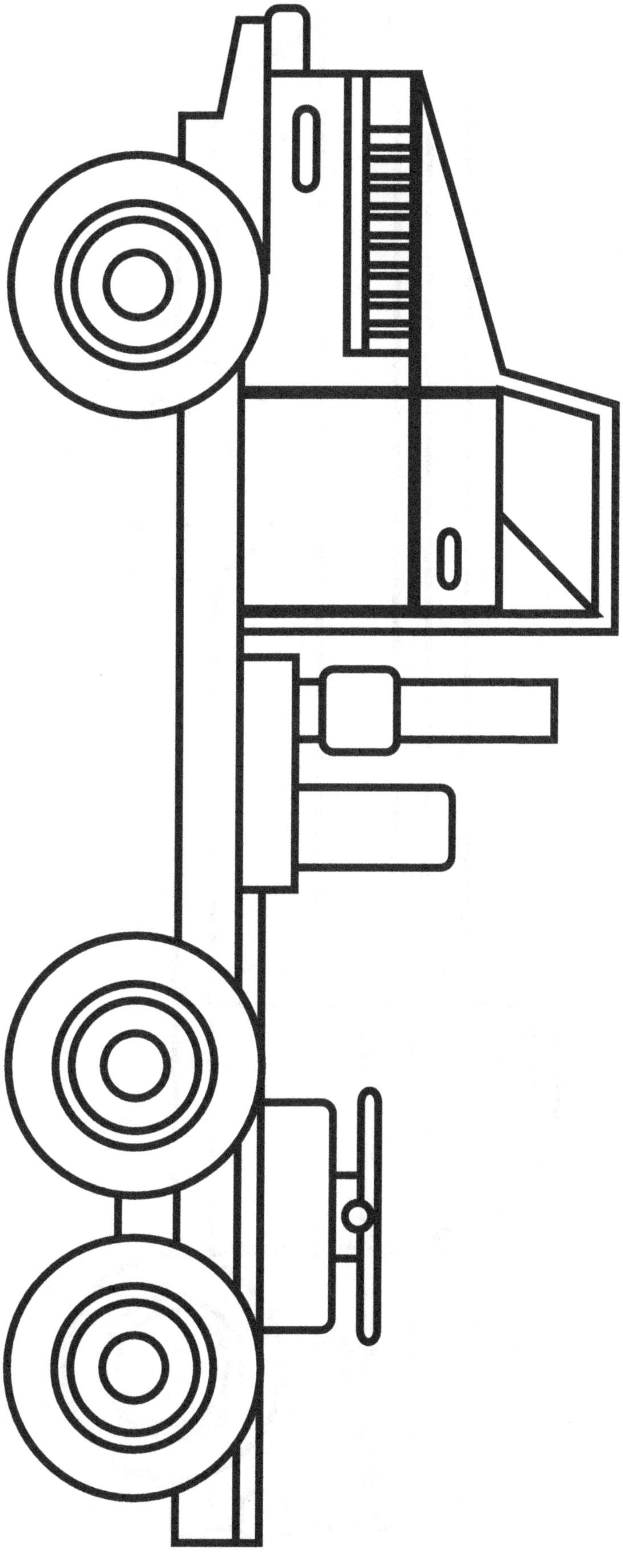

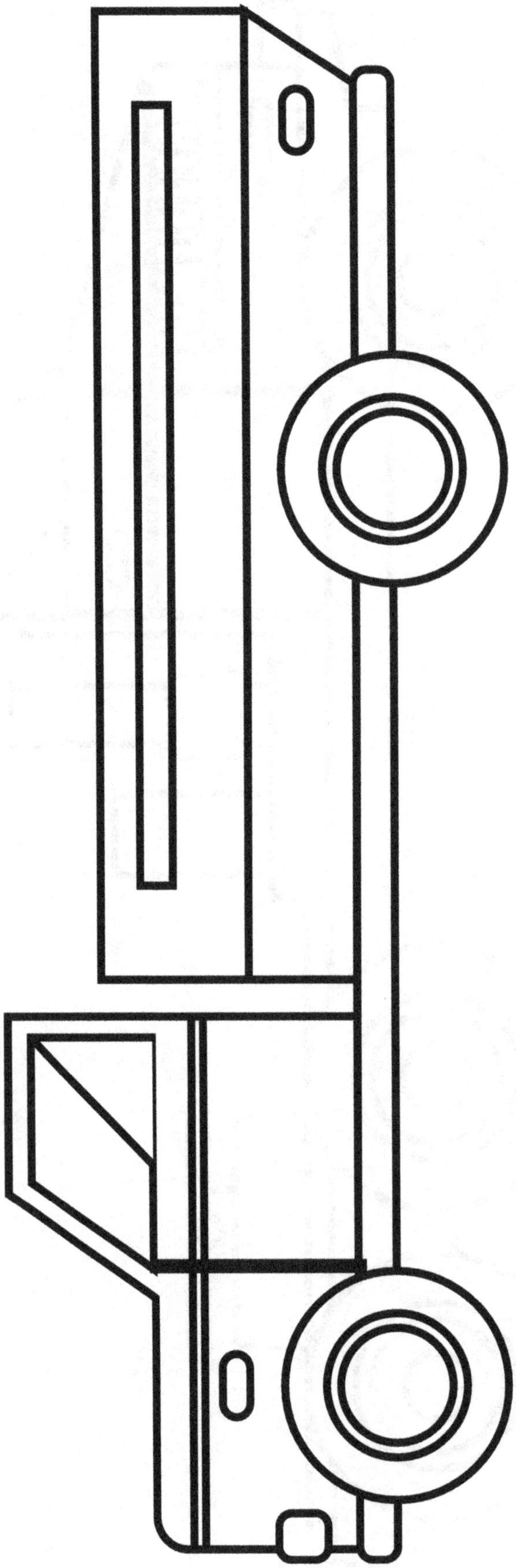

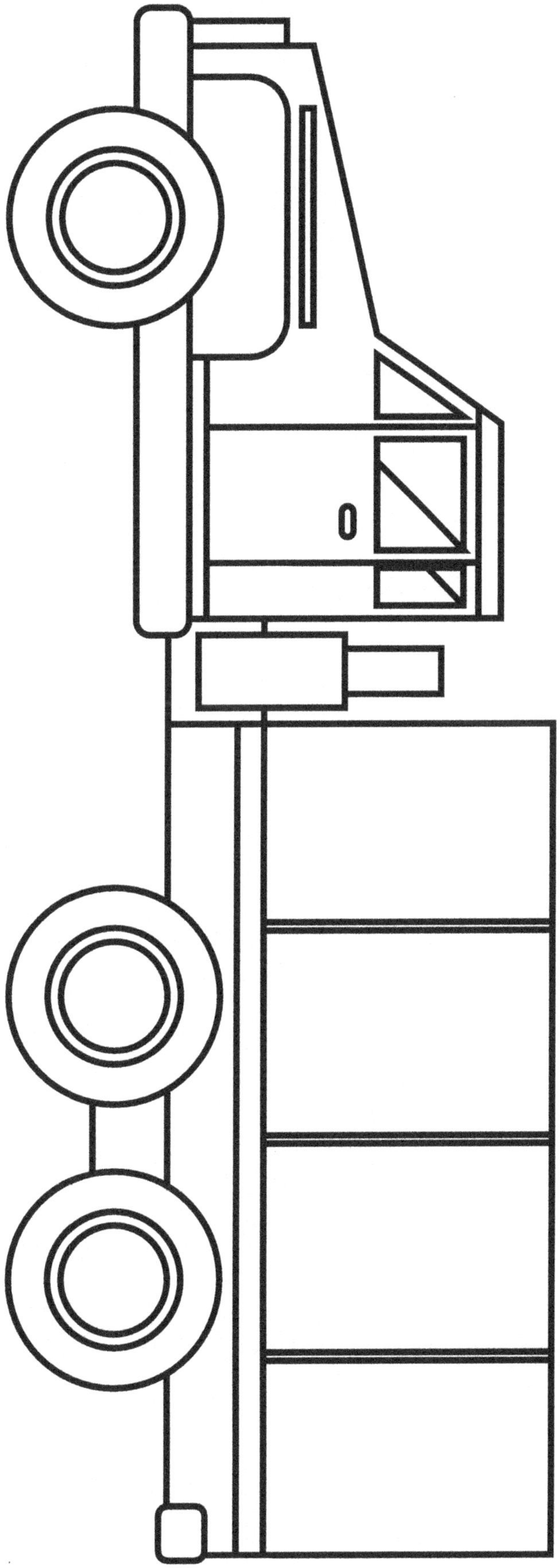

Made in the USA
Monee, IL
27 July 2024

62714157R10059